Transit and Trail Connections: Assessment of Visitor Access to National Wildlife Refuges

December 2010

Photo courtesy of FWS

Photo courtesy of FWS

Prepared for:
U.S. Fish and Wildlife Service
Refuge Roads Program Division of Visitor Services and Communications
Washington, DC

U.S. Department of Transportation
Volpe National Transportation Systems Center

Prepared by:
John A. Volpe National Transportation Systems Center
Research and Innovative Technologies Administration
U.S. Department of Transportation

Acknowledgments

The U.S. Department of Transportation Volpe National Transportation Systems Center (Volpe Center), in coordination with the U.S. Fish and Wildlife Service (FWS), prepared this study with Paul S. Sarbanes Transit in the Parks Program funds.

The Volpe Center would like to thank the following organizations and individuals who graciously provided their time, knowledge and guidance in the development of this report.

Jeff Holm	FWS, Regions 1 and 8
Robert O'Brien	FWS, Region 2
Brandon Jutz	FWS, Region 3
Jo Ann Clark	FWS, Region 4
John Sauer	FWS, Region 5
Jeffrey Mast	FWS, Region 5
Eva Paredes	FWS, Region 6
Troy Civitillo	FWS, Region 7
Nathan Caldwell	FWS

In addition, several individuals and staff from the following agencies and organizations were instrumental in the development of this report:

Archie Carr National Wildlife Refuge

Boyer Chute National Wildlife Refuge

John Heinz National Wildlife Refuge at Tinicum

Kealia Pond National Wildlife Refuge

Minnesota Valley National Wildlife Refuge

Mississippi River Trail, Inc.

Papio Natural Resource District

Rocky Mountain Arsenal National Wildlife Refuge

San Diego National Wildlife Refuge Complex

Shiawassee National Wildlife Refuge

Tualatin River National Wildlife Refuge

Upper Mississippi National Wildlife and Fish Refuge

List of Acronyms

The following terms are used in this report:

CCP   Comprehensive Conservation Plan

COAST   Cooperative Alliance for Seacoast Transportation (Portsmouth, NH)

C-TRAN   Clark County Public Transit Benefit Area Authority

DNR   Minnesota Department of Natural Resources

DOT   Department of Transportation

FWS   U.S. Fish and Wildlife Service

GIS   Geographic Information Systems

LRTP   Long Range Transportation Plan

MARC   Maryland Area Rail Commuter

MOU   Memorandum of Understanding

MRCC   Mississippi River Connections Collaborative

MRT   Mississippi River Trail

MTS   San Diego Metropolitan Transit System

NGO   Non-Governmental Organization

NWR   National Wildlife Refuge

RTC   Regional Transportation Coordinator

RTD   Regional Transit District (Denver, CO)

SANDAG   San Diego Association of Governments

SEPTA   Southeastern Pennsylvania Transportation Authority

TRIP   Paul S. Sarbanes Transit in the Parks

VOTRAN   Volusia County Public Transit System

Table of Contents

Background and Methods

Purpose and Goals

The purpose of the study is to characterize the use of transit and non-motorized transportation modes for visitor access to National Wildlife Refuges (NWRs), as well as identify opportunities for and constraints to alternative transportation access. Specifically, the objectives of the study are to:

1. Identify NWRs with strong existing transit and trail connections, recognizing factors that contribute to the success of using these modes for NWR access

2. Identify sites with high potential for an increased mode shift to transit or non-motorized access, including key partnerships or promotional opportunities to realize these connections

3. Understand how current U.S. Fish and Wildlife (FWS) planning and management decisions affect transit and trail connections to NWRs

4. Provide a tool for FWS staff, partner agencies, and friends groups to recognize potential connections, set priorities for future planning, and ultimately enhance alternative transportation access to NWRs

Study Components

The Transit and Trail Connections Study included the development of a data tool with extensive information about transit and trail connections to many of the most visited NWRs. Study components complement this tool with basic analysis to aid staff, partners, and friends groups with transportation planning and priorities to enhance transit and trail connections. These components include:

- **Priority refuge tables** including information about existing, planned, and high potential transit connections, trail connections, and internal motorized transit service

- **Case studies** of five NWRs with innovative planning or best practices in implementation of transit and/or trail connections

- **Lessons and findings** related to transit and trail connections, barriers to alternative transportation access, and planning for alternative refuge access

- **Recommendations** at the agency and NWR level for next steps to improve transit and trail connections

- A **Matrix** of the results of the quantitative assessment conducted by the Volpe Center team, described in the Methodology section below and featured in the Appendix.

Methodology

The Volpe Center team used the following characteristics of NWRs to create a quantitative assessment of NWRs based on their quality of alternative transportation access. The team assigned a base score of one for each category, with higher scores provided based on better conditions. A matrix of these results can be found in the Appendix:

1. Proximity to urban areas

2. Trail distance

3. Transit distance

4. Trail quality

5. Transit quality

1. *Proximity to urban areas*

Using Geographic Information Systems (GIS) analysis and data from the FWS Service Analysis and the U.S. Census Bureau,[1] the Volpe Center team measured refuge proximity to urban areas, using population size and density to define urban areas. The team assigned ratings to all U.S. refuges based on the following criteria:

- **5** if refuge is within five miles of an urbanized area

- **3** if refuge is within five miles of an urban cluster

- **1** if refuge is not within five miles of an urbanized area or urban cluster

Based on this analysis, the team proceeded to assess transit and trail quality and distance for all refuges with proximity scores of 5 and 3 as well as a few additional refuges identified specifically by FWS staff. The assessment analyzed a total of 142 refuges meeting these urban proximity criteria.[2]

2. *Trail distance*

The team measured the distance of a recreation trail from the postal address of a NWR, on a scale of one to five, based on the following criteria:

- **5** if the trail runs through or terminates at the refuge

- **4** if the trail is one mile or less away from the refuge

- **3** if the trail is between one and two miles away from the refuge

- **2** if the trail is between two and five miles away from the refuge

- **1** if the trail is more than five miles away from the refuge

The analysis primarily utilized Google Maps with recreational trails featured on Google's bicycling directions feature. Bicycle trails listed within Google Maps have been taken from the Rails-to-Trails Conservancy and through user-generated content.

Limitations Of Methodology

Many factors influence people's decisions to use bicycle or pedestrian modes, including but not limited to traffic volume and speed, perception of safety, connectivity, development patterns, demographic characteristics, climate, and supportive policies. The provision of bicycle and pedestrian infrastructure is just one of these factors and is highly dependent on unrelated social and physical factors. In supporting the study purpose of identifying high-potential sites, this methodology seeks to feasibly measure important factors in the use of transit and trails while recognizing that considerations of additional factors will be necessary to better understand the demand for and use of alternative transportation.

3. *Transit distance*

The team measured the distance of the nearest transit stop from the postal address of a NWR, based on the following criteria:

- **5** if transit stop is within 0.25 miles away from the refuge

- **4** if transit stop is between 0.25 miles and 0.5 miles away from the refuge

- **3** if transit stop is between 0.5 miles and one mile away from the refuge

- **2** if transit stop is between one mile and 1.5 miles away from the refuge

- **1** if transit stop is more than 1.5 miles away from the refuge

The analysis used information from transit agency websites and the Google Maps transit feature, where available. For both transit and trail distances, the team verified the relationship between postal addresses and refuge boundaries to confirm the proximity of trails and transit stops to refuges.

4. *Trail quality*

The Volpe Center team measured trail quality on a subjective scale (1 is poor, 2 is fair, 3 is good, 4 is very good, and 5 is excellent) based on the following criteria, using information available from the Rails-to-Trails Conservancy and other recreational trail resources, as available:

- Length of trail

- Surface condition of trail

- Connection to urbanized areas and/or regional destinations (including neighborhoods, schools, other parks and public lands, urban centers, additional trails, etc.)

5. *Transit quality*

The team measured transit quality on a subjective scale (1 is poor, 2 is fair, 3 is good, 4 is very good, and 5 is excellent) based on the following criteria, utilizing information available from transit agencies:

- Frequency of service

- Days per week of service

- Ease of connection (via transit) to other population centers within the region

The Transit and Trails matrix, located in the appendix, contains rankings for each of the analyzed refuges.

Priority Refuges

Introduction

The Priority Refuges section highlights the strongest examples of transit and trail access to National Wildlife Refuges, as uncovered through the research described in the Methodology section. This section also identifies refuges with high potential for new or enhanced transit and trail connections, as well as projects in planning stages, as described by regional U.S. Fish and Wildlife staff. The section is organized by mode (transit or trail), with existing, planned, and potential connections included within each modal section. A full matrix of scores for the 142 evaluated refuges can be found in the Appendix.

Transit

Existing Transit Connections

Volpe Center team evaluated 142 refuges in urban and suburban areas for connections to transit service. The team classified refuges with scores of seven or higher as having strong existing connections, as featured in Table 1. Many refuges with scores below seven have high potential to enhance their existing transit connections, and these are described in Table 2.

Table 1: Refuges with Transit Connections

Refuge		Transit Distance	Transit Quality	Combined Score
1	**Minnesota Valley NWR (MN)** *Region 3*	4 (0.4 miles)	5	9
	Metro Transit's American Boulevard light rail station is connected to the refuge's Bloomington Visitor Center via an off-road, multi-use paved trail. The light rail runs frequently to Minneapolis and other major regional destinations.			
2	**San Diego Bay NWR (CA)** *Region 8*	5 (within refuge)	4	9
	Chula Vista Transit Authority runs a shuttle from the Nature Center (located within the Refuge and operated by a nonprofit organization) to visitor parking near a trolley station and bus stop. San Diego Metropolitan Transit System (MTS) offers transit connections to San Diego and other parts of the region.			
3	**Tijuana Slough NWR (CA)** *Region 8*	5 (0.1 miles)	4	9
	Two San Diego MTS bus routes offer frequent service (15-60 minutes), seven days per week.			
4	**John Heinz NWR at Tinicum (PA)** *Region 5*	4 (0.3 miles)	5	9
	The refuge is located within close proximity to three high-frequency bus routes and two rail transit routes, offering service throughout the Philadelphia region (transit service provided by Southeastern Pennsylvania Transportation Authority (SEPTA)).			
5	**Tualatin River NWR (OR)** *Region 1*	5 (0.05 miles)	4	9
	Tri-Met runs several buses every 15 to 30 minutes, seven days a week, which connect to the greater Portland area.			

Refuge		Transit Distance	Transit Quality	Combined Score
6	**Two Ponds NWR (CO)** *Region 6*	4 (0.5 miles)	4	8
	Denver's Regional Transportation District (RTD) runs three bus routes, seven days a week, within 1.5 miles of this small refuge in a suburb of Denver. The most direct connection is via an express route that serves only during commuting hours.			
7	**Occoquan Bay NWR (VA)** *Region 5*	3 (0.6 miles)	4	7
	The refuge is approximately 25 miles from Washington, D.C., near the Woodbridge Amtrak station, which also serves as a regional hub for four bus routes operating every 30 minutes to two hours. Amtrak service is via the Northeast Regional line.			
8	**Steigerwald Lake NWR (WA)** *Region 1*	4 (0.5 miles)	3	7
	C-TRAN (Clark County Public Transit Benefit Area Authority) has a bus stop one-half mile from the refuge, with buses running every 30 to 60 minutes to the Vancouver, WA area. This refuge is still developing its visitor amenities.			
9	**Wallkill River NWR (NJ/NY)** *Region 5*	5 (Under ¼ miles)	2	7
	The Sussex County Skylands Ride offers commuter-focused bus service very close to the Refuge. High potential to expand service hours to serve refuge visitors.			
10	**Wertheim NWR (NY)** *Region 5*	4 (at entrance)	3	7
	Suffolk County Transit offers a low-frequency bus that stops at the refuge entrance. A Long Island Rail Road station, offering access to New York City and points across Long Island, is less than a mile away.			

Existing Internal Transit

Several high-visitation refuges offer regular shuttle or tram service, often combined with interpretive programs, to allow visitors access to points within the refuge. Other refuges offer these services seasonally, in part to relieve congestion on refuge roads that accompanies high visitation.

- **Santa Ana NWR (TX)**
    - The refuge has a tram system operated in conjunction with the non-profit Valley Nature Center that operates November through April.
- **Seney NWR (MI)**
    - A shuttle bus operates in the summer months, mostly for visitors from retirement homes and senior groups.
- **Ottawa NWR (OH)**
    - This refuge uses the Seney NWR shuttle bus in the winter for interpretive programs.
- **St. Catherine Creek NWR (MS)**
    - Internal tram service.

- **Chincoteague NWR (VA)**

  o An internal tram service operates from late May through September, with the primary purpose of providing beach access from an inland parking lot.

- **Laguna Atacosa NWR (TX)**

  o An internal tram operates from November through March and uses Santa Ana's old trams. The refuge has been awarded a Paul S. Sarbanes Transit in the Parks (Sarbanes) grant in 2010 for funds to upgrade and expand the refuge tram service.

- **J.N. "Ding" Darling NWR (FL)**

  o An internal tram service, operated by a concessionaire, provides 1.5 hour naturalist-led tours of the four-mile Wildlife Drive. Tours operate year-round.

Planned Transit

Several refuges are working with friends groups and transit agencies to enhance existing transit connections or provide new transit service:

- **Rocky Mountain Arsenal NWR (CO)**

  o RTD offers one bus with service 0.3 miles from the refuge entrance (though still far from most visitor amenities), which runs during commuting hours only. Another RTD bus runs with higher frequency but is located one mile from the refuge entrance. The neighboring community of Commerce City completed a study with the Stapleton Development District and found that transit was a viable mode for accessing the refuge's visitor center, currently under construction. The refuge was recently awarded a $400,000 Sarbanes grant to plan an internal transit system.

- **Parker River NWR (MA)**

  o The refuge received a Sarbanes grant in 2010 to purchase a van or shuttle for educational programs, which may also be used to provide access to the refuge from the commuter rail station in Newburyport.

- **Detroit River NWR (MI)**

  o While commuter bus service is currently operating in the area near the refuge, the Southeast Michigan Council of Governments and the Michigan Department of Transportation are in early planning stages for a commuter rail between Detroit and Ann Arbor with a proposed stop two blocks from the Humbug Marsh unit.

- **Kilauea Point NWR (HI)**

  o Kauai Bus offers hourly bus service, six days per week, connecting the town of Kilauea to a bus stop two miles from the refuge. The refuge was awarded a 2010 Sarbanes planning grant to include alternative transportation options in the Kauai NWR Complex CCP, which is currently underway. One proposed alternative is from the provision of a shuttle service between the refuge and Kilauea, the neighboring town.

High Potential Transit Connections

Several refuges are located within the service area of existing transit agencies but are not currently considered to have strong connections. This may be due to low frequency or accessibility of transit service, distance of transit service from refuge visitor amenities, or lack of promotion of transit access. Each of the refuges listed in Table 2 has the potential to benefit greatly from efforts to enhance transit connections.

Table 2: Refuges with High Potential for Transit

Refuge		Transit Distance	Transit Quality	Combined Score
1	**Shiawassee NWR (MI)** *Region 3*	3 (0.6 miles)	3	6
	Saginaw Transit Authority offers regional bus service near the refuge every 40 minutes, six days per week. Partnership efforts would be essential to accustom local residents to use transit.			
2	**Edwin B. Forsythe NWR (NJ)** *Region 5*	3 (0.8 miles)	2	5
	New Jersey Transit (NJ Transit) runs one commuter-focused bus route (hourly frequency, weekdays only) in close proximity to the refuge. Refuge staff could partner with NJ Transit to run weekend service for visitors.			
3	**Chincoteague NWR (VA)** *Region 5*	2 (1.2 miles)	4	6
	The Town of Chincoteague's Island Trolley runs seasonally, seven days per week, to destinations throughout the town. There is potential to enhance this connection through non-motorized improvements or transit service.			
4	**Don Edwards San Francisco Bay NWR (CA)** *Region 8*	2 (1 mile)	3	5
	The Alameda-Contra Costa Transit Agency runs an hourly bus, seven days per week, with connections available to the greater San Francisco Bay area. There is potential to streamline transit connections to allow easier visitor access to the refuge.			
5	**Kealia Pond NWR (HI)** *Region 1*	2 (1.1 miles)	3	5
	Maui Bus offers hourly bus service on two routes, seven days per week, to points around Maui. The closest stop is a little over a mile south of the refuge, although a new visitor center currently under construction could feature direct transit service.			
6	**Nisqually NWR (WA)** *Region 1*	1 (2 miles)	4	5
	Intercity Transit offers high-quality transit service to the Olympia region, but the nearest bus stop is two miles away. There is potential to work with Intercity Transit to offer service closer to the refuge, which has a popular visitor center.			

Several other refuges, with scores of under five, are located within five miles of commuter rail service or within other transit service areas. These refuges may currently be accessible to bicyclists traveling by commuter rail or offer future potential for transit route extensions to serve refuge visitors. These refuges include:

- **Great Swamp NWR (NJ)**

  o NJ Transit offers frequent rail service to Newark and New York City along the Gladstone Branch of its Morristown Line. Six different stations are located within 4.5 miles from the refuge, with the closest in Basking Ridge situated 2.4 miles away. There exists high potential for bikers traveling by commuter rail, although bicycles are not allowed on refuge trails. NJ Transit permits passengers to bring bicycles onto trains, except during rush hours (6:00 to 10 AM and 4:00 to 7:00 PM) and major holidays. Surrounding roads are residential but do not include specific bicycle infrastructure. The refuge permits bicycling on Pleasant Plains Road, a principle auto tour route that is unpaved for most of its length.

- **Stewart B. McKinney NWR (CT)**

  o Estuary Transit offers bus service along Route 1 that make stops based on passenger request, though it is unclear the degree to which this is used for visitor access.

- **Lake Woodruff NWR (FL)**

  o A VOTRAN (Volusia County Public Transit System) bus route passes within one mile of the refuge entrance and headquarters, though the bus route caters to commuters. There may be potential for partnership for visitor transit access.

- **Great Bay NWR (NH)**

  o There may be potential to work with the Cooperative Alliance for Seacoast Transportation (COAST) out of Portsmouth to offer bus service closer to the refuge. The closest stop is currently three miles away.

- **Monomoy NWR (MA)**

  There is potential for seasonal shuttle or transit service to Chatham (with transit connections elsewhere in Cape Cod). In 2010, Monomoy completed an alternative transportation study which considers access options to Chatham in greater detail.

- **San Pablo NWR (CA)**

  o Sonoma County Transit has a commuter bus that travels right past the refuge but does not stop at the entrance.

- **Pinckney Island NWR (SC)**

  o Many Lowcountry Regional Transportation Authority bus routes pass by the refuge entrance as they bring workers on and off Hilton Head Island, but there are no bus stops nearby.[3]

- **Mason Neck NWR (MD)**

  o The refuge is located within a major commuting corridor between Baltimore and Washington, D.C., but the nearest bus and rail lines are at least six miles away in Lorton and Woodbridge.

- **Patuxent Research Refuge (MD)**

  o The refuge is within 5 miles of the Maryland Area Rail Commuter (MARC) train and regional bus service, but the surrounding roads are not hospitable to bicycles, which is a barrier for intermodal connections. The proximity to several major population centers gives this refuge high potential for transit connections.

Trails

Existing Trail Connections

The Volpe Center team evaluated 142 refuges in urban and suburban areas for trail connections. 12 refuges have two or more connections, 23 refuges have one trail connection, and 106 refuges have no trail connections (this includes refuges with no public access or no land access).

The team classified refuges with a score of eight or higher as having strong existing connections, as featured in Table 3. Many refuges with scores below eight have high potential to enhance their existing trail connections, and these are described in Table 4.

Table 3: Refuges with Trail Connections

	Refuge	Trail Distance	Trail Quality	Combined Score
1	**Big Muddy National Fish and Wildlife Refuge (MO)** *Region 3*	5 (within refuge)	5	10
	Katy Trail State Park runs 225 miles along the Missouri River between St. Louis and Boonville. The refuge itself is scattered, composed of small pockets of land along the river between St. Louis and Kansas City. There are plans to connect many of these pockets to Katy Trail State Park.			
2	**Minnesota Valley NWR (MN)** *Region 3*	5 (within refuge)	5	10
	The refuge is connected to trail systems alongside the Minnesota and Mississippi Rivers, which offer links throughout metropolitan Minneapolis-St. Paul.			
3	**San Diego Bay NWR (CA)** *Region 8*	5 (within refuge)	5	
	The 24-mile Bayshore Bikeway loops around the San Diego Bay and connects with the Sweetwater Marsh and South Bay unit of this refuge. The two-mile Sweetwater Bikeway connects to the Bayshore Bikeway approximately one mile north of the Sweetwater Marsh unit.			
4	**Upper Mississippi National Wildlife and Fish Refuge—Savannah District (IL)** *Region 3*	5 (within refuge)	5	10
	The refuge is along the Mississippi River Trail and the 60-mile Great River Trail, which connects to the Quad Cities metropolitan area to the south (population 380,000).			
5	**Assabet River NWR (MA)** *Region 5*	5 (within refuge)	4	9
	The refuge is located along the Assabet River Rail Trail. A recently opened visitor center offers opportunities for visitors to learn more about trail opportunities and connections.			
6	**Big Branch Marsh NWR (LA)** *Region 4*	5 (within refuge)	4	9
	The refuge is located along the 27.5-mile Tammany Trace Bike Trail on the north shore of Lake Pontchartrain.			
7	**Don Edwards San Francisco Bay NWR (CA)** *Region 8*	5 (within refuge)	4	9
	A number of trails along the south end of the San Francisco Bay run within the refuge. A separated bicycle/pedestrian lane exists along the Dunbarton Bridge, which crosses San Francisco Bay through the refuge. The refuge is also connected to the Coyote Hills Regional Park trail network by a bridge over the Dunbarton Bridge Toll Plaza.			
8	**Upper Mississippi National Wildlife and Fish Refuge—La Crosse District (WI)** *Region 3*	5 (within refuge)	4	9
	The refuge is located along the Mississippi River Trail, as well as adjacent to the La Crosse River State Trail (21 miles) and the Great River State Trail (24 miles).			
9	**J.N. "Ding" Darling NWR (FL)** *Region 4*	5 (within refuge)	3	8
	J.N. "Ding" Darling NWR's trail system and Wildlife Drive is connected to the extensive multi-use path system of the City of Sanibel. Sanibel Island has over 26 miles of paved bike trails that cover almost the entire island.			
10	**Pelican Island NWR (FL)** *Region 4*	5 (within refuge)	3	8
	The Jungle Trail (an unpaved road popular for bicyclists and walkers) runs through the refuge, with the Indian River Lagoon National Scenic Byway nearby.			

Refuge	Trail Distance	Trail Quality	Combined Score
11	**Rocky Mountain Arsenal NWR (CO)** *Region 6*	3 (2-4 miles)	5	8
	The refuge is located within two to four miles of numerous trail connections throughout the Denver metropolitan area, including the 13 mile Sand Creek Regional Greenway. Constructed in partnership with Commerce City, the 13-mile Perimeter Trail covers the eastern, northern, and western refuge boundaries and allows bicycle and pedestrian access with potential connections to other regional trails (the Perimeter Trail will cover the 19-mile circumference of the refuge once it is fully constructed).			
12	**Steigerwald Lake NWR (WA)** *Region 1*	5 (within refuge)	3	8
	The Columbia River Dike Trail runs through the refuge and connects to Vancouver, approximately 20 miles to the west.			
13	**Tijuana Slough NWR (CA)** *Region 8*	3 (1.6 miles)	5	8
	The refuge is less than two miles from the Bayshore Bikeway, which loops around the San Diego Bay.			

Additionally, a few refuges featured trails that run close to or within refuge boundaries, but are not easily accessible to official refuge addresses. These refuges include:

- **Great Meadows NWR (MA)**

    o The refuge is along the Reformatory Branch Trail in eastern Massachusetts, which is approximately 2.5 miles away and connects with the Minuteman Bikeway. The Minuteman Bikeway is an 11-mile trail extending into Greater Boston.

- **Upper Mississippi River National Wildlife and Fish Refuge—Winona District (MN)**

    o The refuge is along the 24-mile Great River State Trail on the Wisconsin side of river, as well as the Mississippi River Trail.

- **Horicon NWR (WI)**

    o The refuge is adjacent to the 34-mile Wild Goose State Trail. Visitors can access the refuge from the links spurring off the trail.

Planned Trails

Several refuges are currently designing or constructing future trails to provide or improve access for visitors. Some of these refuges are already accessible by trails, while others feature no existing connections. These refuges are:

- **Boyer Chute NWR (NE)**

    o A project scheduled for completion in 2011 will connect the 1.5 mile gap between the Boyer Chute Trail, which extends south of the refuge to the Washington County line, and the Omaha Riverfront Trail, which travels northward from Omaha along the Missouri River.

- **Chincoteague NWR (VA)**

    o A project is currently under construction for a half-mile multi-use trail to connect the refuge with the town of Chincoteague using Sarbanes funds.

- **Eastern Shore of Virginia NWR (VA)**

  o A three mile bike trail connecting Kiptopeke State Park with the Eastern Shore of Virginia NWR is currently under construction. The effort is a partnership between the refuge and the Virginia Department of Conservation and Recreation.

- **Minnesota Valley NWR (MN)**

  o The Minnesota Valley NWR, in addition to its strong existing connections, could soon be connected by a unified trail system along the Minnesota River connecting southern suburbs with Minneapolis city bike trails. The project has strong support from the involved communities.

- **National Elk Refuge (WY)**

  o A bicycle and pedestrian trail is currently being built from the Interagency Visitor Center in Jackson to the Grand Teton National Park sign pull-out in the right-of-way along US Highway 89 North. The trail segment is due to open in 2011 using Sarbanes funds. It will be part of a 20 mile off-road route from Jenny Lake in Grand Teton National Park, through the National Elk Refuge, and into the town of Jackson.

- **Neil Smith NWR (IA)**

  o The Neil Smith NWR in Prairie City recently received a Sarbanes grant to complete construction of a bicycle/pedestrian trail between its visitor center and the Plainsmen Trail in the neighboring community of Prairie City. Additionally, plans are under consideration for a rail-trail between Prairie City and Des Moines, 20 miles to the west.

- **Rocky Mountain Arsenal NWR (CO)**

  o While already connected to the Denver metropolitan area through nearby bicycle trails, the refuge has current plans under consideration to provide a direct connection between the visitor center and the Denver region. In the future there will be a system of trails throughout the refuge.

- **Wichita Mountains NWR (OK)**

  o A project is already underway to widen shoulders for recreational bicycling along roads leading to the Wichita Mountains NWR from the gateway communities of Cache, Medicine Park and neighboring Ft. Sill, the Army's main artillery training base. The refuge, its friends groups, and outlying communities are working together on a plan to improve recreational opportunities for visitors by developing trails and improving roads for bicycling safety on the refuge.

High Potential Trail Connections

Several refuges have strong potential trail connections to outlying areas. These potential connections could include the extension of a nearby trail, connections of nearby trails with one another, the construction of new trails to urban areas, or the construction of infrastructure to bypass barriers such as highways and rivers. Each of the refuges listed in Table 4 (see page 12) has the potential to benefit greatly from efforts to enhance trail connections.

Table 4: Refuges with High Potential for Trail Connections

Refuge	Trail Distance	Trail Quality	Combined Score
1 **Shiawassee NWR (MI)** *Region 3*	5 (within refuge)	2	7
Already adjacent to the Saginaw Valley Rail Trail, the refuge is on the outskirts of Saginaw (population 55,000). While visitor access by bicycle and pedestrian modes is high, there no formal connections between the refuge and the city. Roads in the area are considered to be in poor condition for bicycling.			
2 **John Heinz NWR at Tinicum (PA)** *Region 5*	5 (within refuge)	2	7
Situated in the heart of the Philadelphia metropolitan area, this refuge lacks any formal trail connections with the outlying area. A local nongovernmental organization conducted a feasibility study on improving non-motorized access in 2007, though the feasible alternative has yet to be implemented (see case study).			
3 **Archie Carr NWR (FL)** *Region 4*	4 (0.5 miles)	3	7
Along the Florida's Atlantic coast, the refuge is close to the Pelican Island NWR and only 0.5 miles away from the Jungle Trail. A multi-use path runs alongside the Indian River Lagoon National Scenic Byway within the refuge.			
4 **John H. Chafee NWR (RI)** *Region 5*	4 (0.5 miles)	3	7
A major highway separates the William C. O'Neill Bike Path in Wakefield (6.1 miles long, and near the University of Rhode Island) from the refuge.			
5 **St. Marks NWR (FL)** *Region 4*	2 (2 miles)	5	7
The Big Bend National Scenic Byway was recently designated by the FHWA and included the refuge's entry road that connects with the historic lighthouse, a major draw for visitors. However, a river separates the refuge from the town of St. Marks and the 20-mile Tallahassee-St. Marks Historic Railroad Trail.			
6 **Mountain Longleaf NWR (AL)** *Region 4*	2 (4.3 miles)	4	6
The 33-mile Chief Ladiga Trail lies to the northwest of the NWR. The refuge is relatively new with limited visitor facilities. Refuge staff could seek to connect with the trail as the refuge expands access.			
7 **Monomoy NWR (MA)** *Region 5*	2 (4.8 miles)	4	6
The 22-mile Cape Cod Rail Trail, which runs throughout Cape Cod, features a spur into the town of Chatham. The spur ends roughly five miles from the refuge entrance. This area sees high visitation in the summer months.			
8 **McNary NWR (WA)** *Region 1*	2 (2 miles)	3	5
The refuge is located near the Tri-Cities area, and the new environmental education center is located approximately two miles from a connection to the Benton-Franklin bicycle and pedestrian infrastructure network. This network provides hundreds of miles of off-road trails, bicycle lanes, sidewalks, and other infrastructure connected to cities throughout the region.			
9 **Patuxent Research Refuge (MD)** *Region 5*	2 (3.5 miles)	3	5
There are no connections between the refuge and the Washington, Baltimore, and Annapolis trails in Prince Georges and Anne Arundel counties.			
10 **Nisqually NWR (WA)** *Region 1*	2 (4.9 miles)	2	4
An eastward extension of Woodward Trail would open access to the refuge from Olympia.			

Case Studies

Minnesota Valley National Wildlife Refuge

Refuge Background: The Minnesota Valley National Wildlife Refuge (NWR), headquartered in Bloomington, Minnesota, covers 14,000 acres and spans 99 miles of the Minnesota River. A focal point for visitors is the newly renovated Bloomington Visitor Center, located approximately ten miles south of downtown Minneapolis. The refuge offers wildlife observation, environmental education, and recreational amenities to approximately 300,000 annual visitors. Approximately 80 percent of visitors are residents of the greater Twin Cities metropolitan area, which was home to approximately 3.3 million people in 2009.[4] The Visitor Center is located off American Boulevard, a two-lane, paved road with a landscaped median, a sidewalk on the north/west side, and a separated multi-use paved path on the south/east side. The multi-use path links to the greater Twin Cities bicycle network[5] and many regional destinations. Visitors can walk directly from American Boulevard to the Visitor Center on separated paved paths.

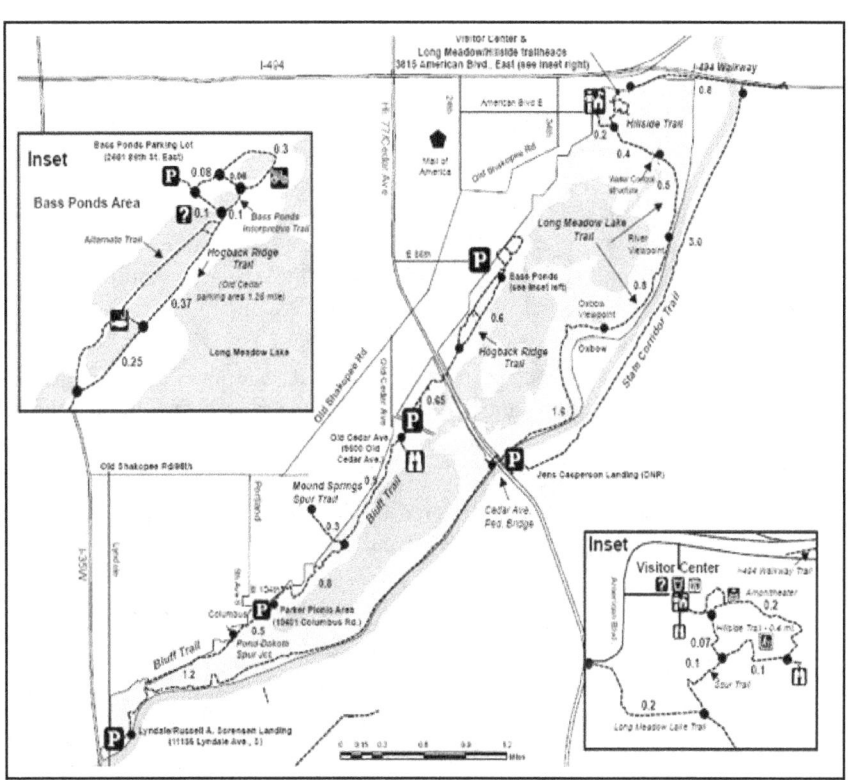

Refuge map, displaying parking areas and internal trails

Map courtesy of FWS

Transit Connections: Minnesota Valley's close proximity to the new Hiawatha Line light rail service provides access to points across the Twin Cities region. Metro Transit, the Twin Cities' transit agency, opened its America Boulevard Station in December 2009, which is located 0.4 miles from the Visitor Center entrance. The station offers light rail service to downtown Minneapolis, the Mall of America, the Minneapolis-St. Paul International Airport, and the Northstar commuter rail line, with future connections planned to St. Paul. The light rail runs seven days a week with frequencies of 10 to 15 minutes, from 4 a.m. to 1 a.m. The light rail connection has opened access to the refuge for inner-city residents and other underserved populations. In addition to the light rail, numerous bus routes serve the Mall of America, located approximately one mile west of the Visitor Center. Metro Transit Route 54 runs every 15 to 30 minutes and stops one-half mile from the Visitor Center as well.

Trail Connections: The seven-county Twin Cities region has an extensive network of bicycle lanes and off-road bicycle trails, supported by a strong local culture for cycling.

- American Boulevard's multi-use trail connects to the Mall of America, the City of Bloomington, and other suburbs on the east side of the Minnesota River. The multi-use trail also connects to the Mississippi River Trail and downtown Minneapolis.

- The 27-mile Southwest Regional Light Rail Transit Trail terminates at the Louisville Swamp Unit of the refuge.

- The Minnesota Valley State Trail and several unnamed trails run along the Mississippi and Minnesota Rivers, offering non-motorized access to refuge units from surrounding urban and suburban areas. Refuge staff is supporting the Minnesota Department of Natural Resources' (DNR) efforts to develop the Minnesota Valley State Trail to connect units of the refuge with each other. The refuge, as well as many outlying commuties, are coordinating with DNR in support of their multi-use trail projects.

- DNR is in pre-planning stages of a project to develop a trail through the Long Meadow Lake Unit of the refuge that would connect suburbs south of the refuge to the regional bike network.

Promotion: The refuge website lists directions to the Bloomington Visitor Center from light rail and bus. The Metro Transit website has a Trip Planner feature that allows users to map a transit route to the Bloomington Visitor Center. As both the light rail and the Visitor Center are relatively new/recently re-opened, promotional efforts have not yet been fully developed. Refuge staff also promote transit informally to school groups, informing students and their parents that they can travel to the refuge by light rail. In the future, refuge staff hope to partner with Refuge Friends, Inc. (the refuge's friends group) to install an informational kiosk at the American Boulevard Station and display advertisements about the refuge in trains and buses.

Lessons: The Refuge has been partnering with State and local governments to diversify access and, taking advantage of their urban location, to connect urban youth with the refuge. In Minnesota Valley, non-motorized transportation projects emerge through community activism. For example, several Minnesota off-road biking clubs and birding clubs worked together to build the political will and identify funding for enhanced trail access. Like other urban refuges, refuge staff cite the challenge of balancing the needs of wildlife and people. Staff members strive to maintain the integrity of the habitat with the fact that visitors love the refuge and continually take advantage of its amenities.

The Hiawatha Light Rail offers service within walking
distance of the Visitor Center.

Image courtesy of Metro Transit

San Diego Bay and Tijuana Slough National Wildlife Refuges

Refuge Background: The San Diego Bay and Tijuana Slough National Wildlife Refuges both lie in densely populated areas south of downtown San Diego, attracting nearly 75,000 combined visitors in 2009. The San Diego Bay NWR is comprised of two units, Sweetwater Marsh and South Bay, which are composed of remaining salt marsh and coastal uplands in the heavily developed San Diego Bay area.

The Chula Vista Nature Center at Sweetwater Marsh, run by a partnership of a nonprofit group, the City of Chula Vista, and the San Diego Bay NWR, offers interpretive and interactive attractions for visitors. The Nature Center parking lot is located at the western end of E Street, a four-lane arterial at the intersection of Interstate 5, where visitors can park and board a shuttle bus that departs approximately every 15 minutes and operates between the parking area and the Nature Center. A small parking lot for the South Bay unit is located at the northern end of 13th Street in Imperial Beach, a two-lane paved access road off of the six-lane, median-separated Palm Avenue.

The Tijuana Slough NWR is a salt marsh nestled between the city of Imperial Beach and the Mexican border. The refuge maintains essential habitats for many migrating shorebirds and waterfowl along the Pacific Flyway, a major route of travel for migratory birds. The refuge is included in the Tijuana River National Estuarine Reserve, designated by the National Oceanic and Atmospheric Administration. The Reserve is locally administered by the California State Parks System, which leases land from the Fish and Wildlife Service for the Tijuana Esturary Visitor. The Estuary Visitor Center is located on Caspian Way, a two-lane paved access road off of the high-traffic, four-lane Imperial Beach Boulevard. At the end of Seacoast Drive there is also a wildlife viewing deck and interpretive panels.

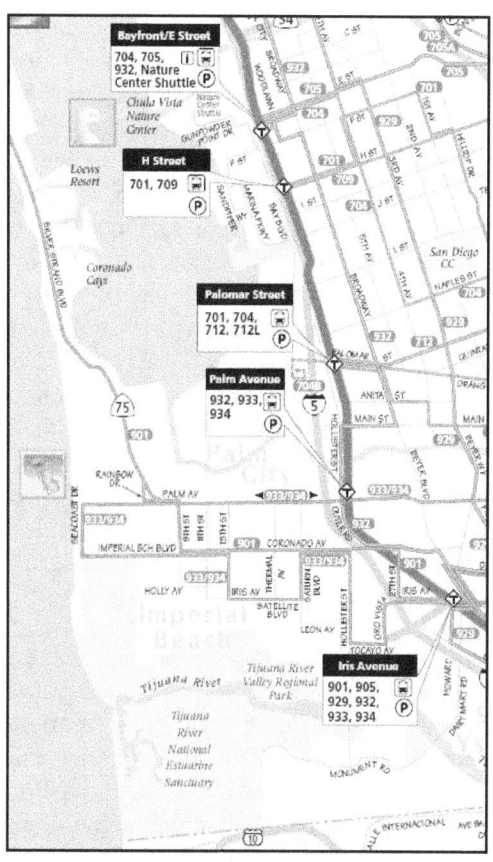

MTS transit map of the area
Map courtesy of the Metropolitan Transit System

Transit Connections: Visitors can access each refuge through trolley and bus connections.

- Blue Line trolley-style light rail service through the Metropolitan Transit System's (MTS) San Diego Trolley connects visitors of the Sweetwater Marsh unit of the San Diego Bay NWR to the Bayfront/E Street station. The shuttle bus that offers service to the Chula Vista Nature Center (upon passenger request) departs from the Nature Center parking lot, 0.2 miles west of the trolley station. The Blue Line operates between the Old Town neighborhoods of San Diego and San Ysidro, approximately 15 miles south of San Diego along the Mexican border. Travel time between the Bayfront/E Street station and downtown San Diego is approximately 15 minutes, with trolleys departing every 15 minutes on weekends and weekdays outside of rush hour.

- Visitors can also access MTS bus service to the South Bay unit of the San Diego Bay NWR and to Tijuana Slough NWR at the Palm Avenue and Iris Avenue Blue Line stations. Bus routes 933 and 934 run in reverse directions (clockwise/counterclockwise) along Palm Avenue, with a stop at 13th Street two blocks south of the South Bay Unit parking area, and Imperial Beach Boulevard, with a stop at 3rd Street one block north of the Tijuana Estuary Visitor Center. Buses depart from the two stations every 12 to 15 minutes on weekdays, every 20 to 30 minutes on weekends.[6]

Trail Connections: Visitors can reach both units of the San Diego Bay NWR via the Bayshore Bikeway, a 24-mile bikeway around the San Diego Bay from Coronado to downtown San Diego. The route, currently comprised of 13 miles of off-road trails and 11 miles of on-road bike lanes, provides direct access to the Chula Vista Nature Center shuttle bus parking lot. The City of San Diego, with assistance from the San Diego Bay NWR and the San Diego Association of Governments (SANDAG), recently completed construction of a segment of the trail adjacent to the South Bay unit, providing visitors with outstanding views of the refuge.[7] San Diego Bay NWR refuge staff indicated that many visitors utilize the Bayshore Bikeway to visit the South Bay unit, as well as to access the Chula Vista Nature Center, which offers bicycle racks in its shuttle bus parking lot. An additional multi-use trail along the eastern edge of the South Bay unit offers access to the Bayshore Bikeway from Palm Avenue. Finally, the two-mile Sweetwater Bikeway connects to the Bayshore Bikeway approximately one mile north of the Sweetwater March unit. The Tijuana Estuary Visitor Center also contains bicycle racks for visitors.

Promotion: Both refuges actively promote alternative transportation services in promotional materials (such as brochures) for refuge events. Refuge staff observed that events at the Tijuana Slough NWR draw many visitors using bus access. The MTS website also lists the Chula Vista Nature Center as a point of interest in the area. Additionally, the San Diego Bay NWR website encourages visitors to utilize the Bayshore Bikeway at the South Bay unit. Through its promotion of alternative transportation, both refuges are hoping to increase recreational opportunities in urban areas and contribute to the improved livability of the region.

Map of the Bayshore Bikeway around San Diego Bay
Map courtesy of SANDAG

Lessons: The unique location of these refuges within a dense metropolitan area has helped the San Diego Bay and Tijuana Slough NWRs emerge as national leaders in utilizing alternative transportation to serve visitors. Both refuges have leveraged existing trolley and bus connections to encourage visitors to utilize public transportation when visiting the refuges. By offering shuttle service to the Chula Vista Nature Center upon passenger request at the Bayfront/E Street station, transit visitors are able to conveniently experience the Nature Center and the Sweetwater Marsh unit of the San Diego Bay NWR. The San Diego Bay NWR's partnership with the City of San Diego and SANDAG to construct a segment of the Bayshore Bikeway adjacent to the South Bay unit reflects the refuge and region's commitment to offer innovative interpretive experiences using recreation. These and other efforts have helped make each refuge accessible to a large portion of San Diego area residents using alternative transportation.

John Heinz National Wildlife Refuge at Tinicum

Refuge Background: The John Heinz National Wildlife Refuge (NWR) at Tinicum is located in southwest Philadelphia. The Philadelphia metropolitan area had a population of approximately 5.9 million. [8] The 1,200 acre refuge contains a freshwater tidal wetland and is home to more than 300 species of birds and other wildlife. The refuge attracts approximately 130,000 visitors annually. Visitor amenities include recreational trails, canoeing routes, fishing and wildlife viewing platforms, and the Cusano Environmental Education Center. The refuge access road is paved with no designated pedestrian or bicycle facilities. The main entrance to the refuge is along Lindbergh Boulevard at 86th Street; both streets are paved, two-lane roads in multifamily residential neighborhoods. Lindbergh Boulevard has sidewalks along its eastern side, and a wide shoulder that can accommodate cyclists. Visitors would likely use South 84th Street to access Lindbergh Boulevard. 84th Street is a six-lane, arterial road with a landscaped median and bicycle lanes in both directions.

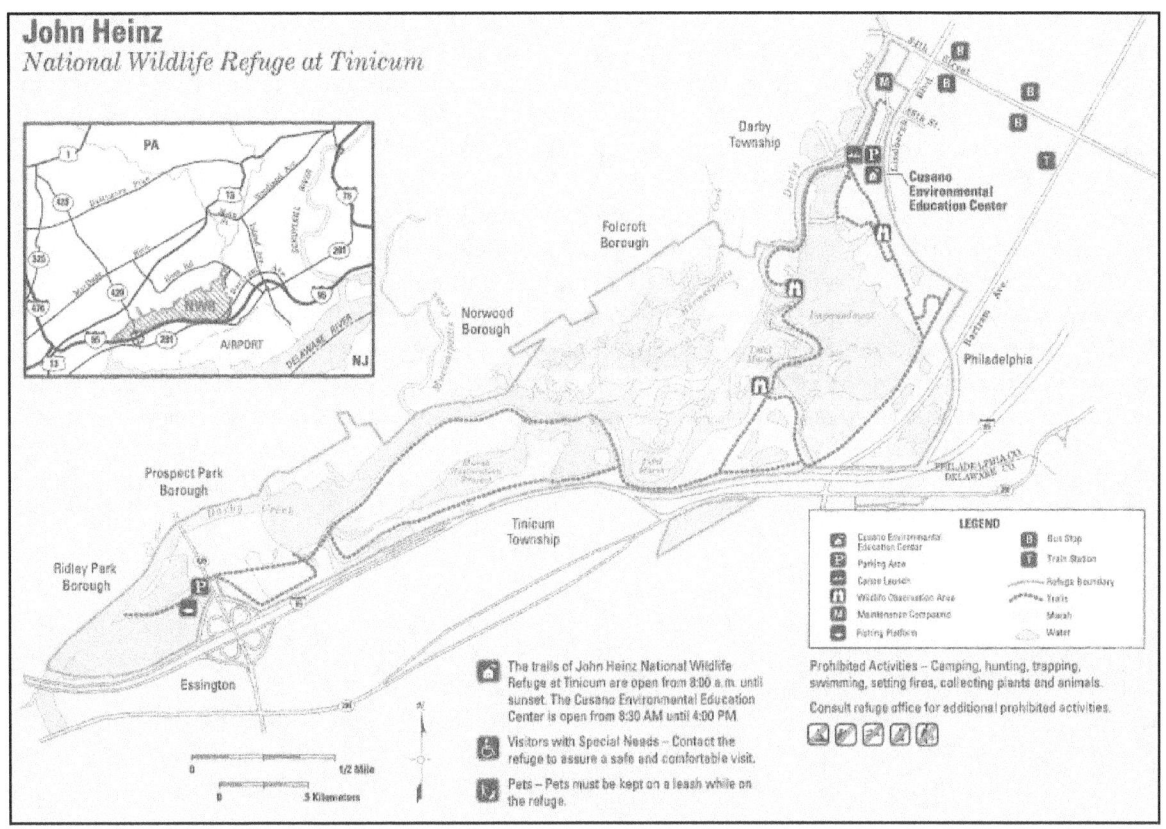

Refuge map, displaying parking areas and internal trails

Map courtesy of FWS

Transit Connections: Located less than seven miles from downtown Philadelphia and adjacent to the Philadelphia International Airport, the John Heinz NWR is accessible via several transit routes run by the Southeastern Pennsylvania Transportation Authority (SEPTA). SEPTA offers regional rail, light rail, bus, trolley, and paratransit service with approximately 240 million passenger rides in 2009.[9] Visitors can access SEPTA bus routes 37, 108, and 422/423 (Airport Line) from a bus stop at Lindbergh Boulevard and 84th Street, located 0.3 miles from the refuge entrance and 0.5 miles from the Education Center. Additionally, the Eastwick Station is located one mile from the Education Center and offers service on the Route 36 Trolley to Downtown and West Philadelphia. The Sharon Hill Station is approximately 1.5 miles from the Education Center and offers SEPTA Regional Rail service between downtown Philadelphia and Wilmington, Delaware.

Trail Connections: Sidewalks, bicycle lanes, and wide shoulders line the primary roads accessing the refuge. Although bicycle lanes connect 84th Street and Lindbergh Boulevard to downtown Philadelphia and surrounding neighborhoods, bicycle infrastructure is not continuous. The refuge is located along the East Coast Greenway, a developing trail system covering 3,000 miles from Canada to Florida. The Greenway passes through the refuge, entering on Lindberg Boulevard to the north and exiting through Route 420 to the south. In 2007, the Clean Air Council (a Philadelphia-based nonprofit environmental advocacy organization) completed a study examining three feasible alternatives for improved pedestrian and bicycle access to the refuge. The study found that the construction of an off-road trail from the SEPTA Eastwick Station to the east entrance of the refuge would provide the greatest improvement for the lowest cost, though access is contingent upon funding and land acquisition. [10] The Clean Air Council is also pursuing a connection between the refuge and the planned multi-use Cobbs Creek Connector trail.

Promotion: FWS staff promotes transit informally through conversations with refuge visitors and outreach to school groups. According to staff, a large number of Philadelphia-area residents do not own cars, and transit offers a cost-effective means to access the refuge. The refuge website contains access information for the Route 37 and 108 buses and the Eastwick Station Regional Rail, as well as providing a link to SEPTA's website, which has a Trip Planner feature that shows visitors how to navigate to the refuge by transit. The refuge informally partners with SEPTA, through participation in joint community or refuge events, to promote transit connections. The refuge also often hosts meetings run by the Clean Air Council and other non-governmental organizations (NGOs) related to non-motorized access studies.

Lessons: John Heinz NWR at Tinicum is able to offer visitors an accessible opportunity to interact with wildlife within an urban area. The refuge staff relies upon NGO partner agencies, including the Clean Air Council, to lead promotion and research of transit and non-motorized connections. While refuge staff promotes bicycle access to the refuge, they try to limit bicycle use within the refuge to small groups or individual use for wildlife viewing purposes. The staff notes a challenge in maintaining bicycle compatibility with the refuge's mission; one way they address this is through the provision of bicycle racks at the visitor center so that cyclists can park their bikes and walk on refuge trails. Refuge partners also cite the constant need to raise money and awareness for non-motorized and transit connections.

Tualatin River National Wildlife Refuge

Refuge Background: The Tualatin River National Wildlife Refuge comprises over 2,000 acres within the floodplain of the Tualatin River basin near Sherwood, Oregon, approximately 15 miles southwest of Portland. The refuge's habitats include rivers and streams, seasonal and forested wetlands, riparian areas, grasslands, and forested uplands. It is an important area for migratory birds, including wintering waterfowl, migrating shorebirds, and breeding and nesting songbirds.[11] The refuge is home to nearly 200 species of birds, over 50 species of mammals, 25 species of reptiles and amphibians, and a wide variety of insects, fish and plants. The refuge has also become a place where people can experience and learn about wildlife and the places they call home. Established in 1992 with strong community support, the refuge opened to the public in 2006 and a new Wildlife Center opened in 2008. Visitors can also make use of the refuge's nature trails, wildlife observation overlooks, and river

Wintering waterfowl at the refuge
Photo courtesy of FWS

overlook.[12] Located off of Oregon Route 99W, a regional highway with two lanes in each direction, the nearly two million residents of the Portland metropolitan area have easy access to the refuge from the city center. Nearly 87,000 people visited the refuge in 2009.

Transit Connections: TriMet, Portland's public transportation provider, offers a bus route with service from downtown Portland to the refuge entrance, where visitors can walk along a short paved path to the Wildlife Center. Route 12 runs from Gresham (approximately 12 miles east of downtown) to downtown Portland before traveling west along Route 99W to Sherwood, with a stop at the refuge along the way. The route runs seven days a week, departing approximately every 15 to 20 minutes. Travel time from SW 5th and Morrison Streets in downtown Portland to the refuge entrance in just under one hour.[13]

Trail Connections: Although the Wildlife Center parking lot contains bicycle racks, accessing the Center on bicycle is difficult. Route 99W, the entry road leading to the refuge, is not marked with bicycle lanes and vehicles travel at high speeds. Although the refuge staff indicate that some bicyclists access the refuge along Route 99W, staff observe more bicycle access is seen at a secondary entrance on the western edge of the refuge along Roy Rogers Road. This entrance is in close proximity to segments of Sherwood's parks system and attracts many families on bicycles. Bicycles are not permitted on refuge trails.

Promotion: The Tualatin River National Wildlife Refuge encourages access using alternative transportation in order to reach out to a larger group of potential visitors. Information on reaching the refuge by bicycle or bus is available on the refuge's profile page and the main refuge website. Refuge staff indicated that they heavily promote alternative transportation, particularly public transportation, in brochures, leaflets, and other outreach materials. Refuge staff actively target populations with limited or no access to a motor vehicle in these efforts, aiming to drive visitation and support within these populations. Additionally, TriMet's website allows visitors to search for travel directions to the refuge easily from its home page. The agency's trip planner provides step-by-step directions to access the refuge bus stop, with information on fares and expected travel times.

Lessons: With the Portland area residents' penchant for recreational activities and TriMet's strong ridership, the Tualatin River National Wildlife Refuge works hard to attract visitation using alternative transportation. By providing information about public transportation, supplementing it with information about where residents can best access the bus route in downtown Portland, and notifying site visitors of locations of bicycle racks, the Tualatin River National Wildlife Refuge actively promotes public transportation services to its attractions.

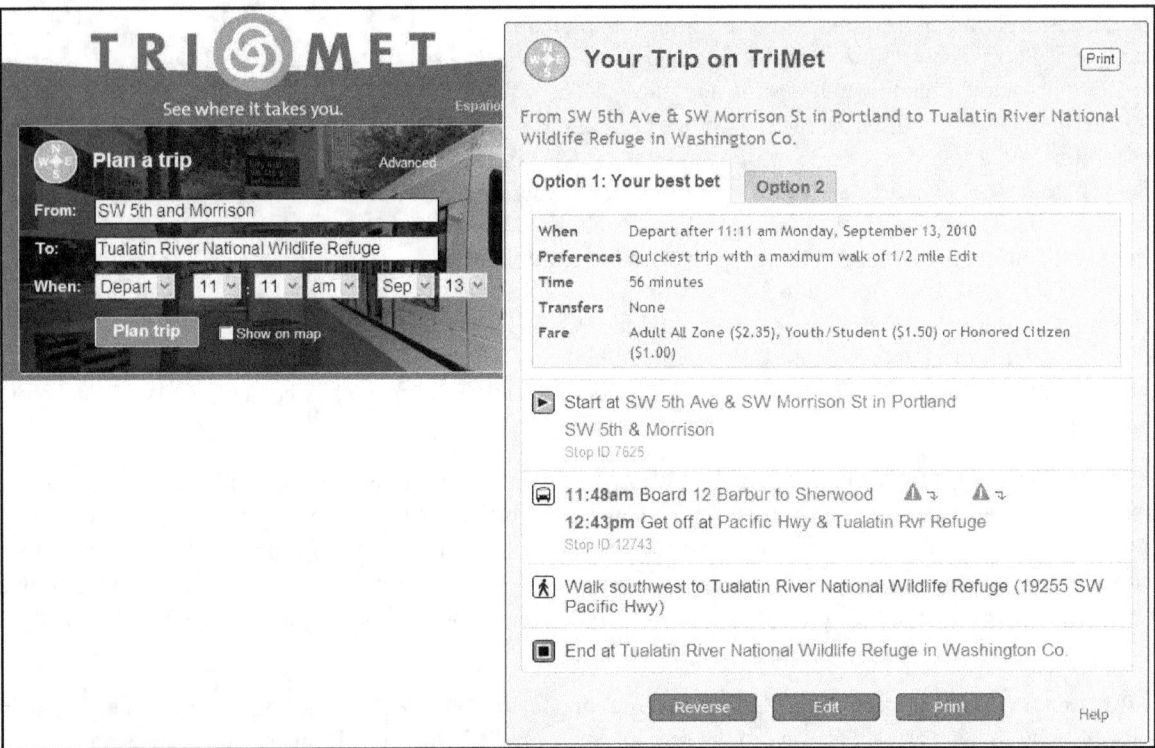

Screenshot of TriMet's trip planner, as featured on its home page.

Courtesy of the Tri-County Metropolitan Transportation District of Oregon

Upper Mississippi River National Wildlife and Fish Refuge

Refuge Background: The Upper Mississippi River National Wildlife and Fish Refuge spans 261 linear miles and over 240,000 acres of the Mississippi River floodplain between Wabasha, Minnesota, and Rock Island, Illinois. It was established in 1924 as a refuge and breeding ground for migratory birds, game animals, and aquatic life, as well as for the conservation of wildflowers and aquatic plants. The refuge has long been a popular attraction, drawing over one million visitors annually for fishing and water-based recreation each, as well as 300,000 additional visits for wildlife observation. The refuge covers four states, 19 counties, and 70 communities and features numerous access points along roads and waterways. The refuge is bordered on both sides by the Great River Road National Scenic Byway. Major cities near the refuge include the Quad Cities of Illinois (East Moline, Moline, and Rock Island) and Iowa (Bettendorf and Davenport); Dubuque, Iowa; La Crosse, Wisconsin; and Winona, Minnesota, home to the refuge headquarters.[14]

Location of the Upper Mississippi River National Wildlife and Fish Refuge

Courtesy of FWS

Transit Connections: The refuge features multiple entry points, owing to its dispersed nature. Accordingly, this situation, along with the rural nature of many refuge areas, limits the ability of transit agencies to directly serve the refuge. Transit agencies serving cities near the refuge include the La Crosse (WI) Municipal Transit Utility, the Winona (MN) Transit Service, the Quad Cities MetroLINK (Rock Island, IL), the Davenport (IA) Citibus, and KeyLine Transit (Dubuque, IA). However, none of these agencies actively promote transit to the refuge on their websites due to the lack of transit services. Opportunities to utilize transit to visit facilities along the refuge outside of these cities is limited and logisitically challenging.

Trail Connections: The Upper Mississippi River National Wildlife and Fish Refuge features many multi-use trails along its length.

- The Great River State Trail is a 24-mile trail through the communities of Onalaska and Trempealeau, Wisconsin, at the northern end of the refuge. Maintained by the Wisconsin Department of Natural Resources, six miles of the trail are within the refuge between Black River and Halfway Creek.[15]

- The Great River Trail in Illinois extends 60 miles along the Mississippi River between Rock Island and Savanna. FWS identifies 13 of the trail's 60 miles as running through the refuge.[16] The trail is part of the nearly 500-mile Grand Illinois Trail extending throughout the state and maintained by the Illinois Department of Natural Resources.[17]

- Other trails near the refuge include the La Crosse River State Trail in Wisconsin, the Heritage Trail north of Dubuque, IA, the Galena River Trail south of Galena, IL, and the Duck Creek Parkway in Davenport and Bettendorf, IA.

In addition to these local and state trails, the Mississippi River Trail (MRT) is engaged in an ongoing effort to provide nearly 3,000 miles of bike-friendly roads and multi-use pathways along both sides of the Mississippi River. The trail is still largely under development, with only small segments designated and signed (one such section being the Great River Trail in Illinois), and the rest existing as local roads along the river. Once complete, the MRT will connect visitors with recreational opportunities within and near the Upper Mississippi River National Wildlife and Fish Refuge.

Promotion: The refuge is working with the MRT to further develop trail infrastructure and encourage use of existing segments. This includes positioning the MRT as a family-friendly alternative to driving, as well as providing convenient parking and access areas for the MRT. The Mississippi River Connections Collaborative, a partnership of local, state, and federal refuge, park, and trail managers, as well as non-profit institutions, is working to develop and promote physical and thematic connections to the river. The refuge also promotes connections with the Great River State Trail in Wisconsin and the Great River Trail in Illinois on its website. Additionally, the website highlights launching points for canoes with route distances and level of difficulty for suggested trips.

Lessons: Unlike many other refuges in this report, the Upper Mississippi River National Wildlife and Fish Refuge features multiple access points in which to enter the refuge. As such, improving transit to specific points along the refuge would only reach a small percentage of visitors. However, a system of multi-use trails lining the refuge would provide visitors countless opportunities to experience different parts of the refuge over many visits. By coordinating efforts with advocacy groups and promoting existing trails along the refuge, the Upper Mississippi River National Wildlife and Fish Refuge is attempting to make that vision a reality.

Great River State Trail in Wisconsin crossing the Black River

Photo courtesy of the Wisconsin Department of Natural Resources

Findings

The findings contained in this section are based on the analysis of transit and trail connections and conversations with Washington Office National Wildlife Refuge System staff and Regional Transportation Coordinators (RTCs). The findings have been categorized into transit, trails, planning, and additional findings.

Transit Findings

Transit connections allow refuges to improve outreach to underserved populations. FWS has been trying to increase refuge visitation for minority, low-income, student, and mobility-impaired populations. The low visitation rates from these groups can be attributed, in part, to their lower rates of car ownership. Transit service allows underserved populations to independently visit refuges by bus or light rail. Some refuge staff also encourage students on field trips to return to the refuge via transit with their families.

Many potential transit connections in suburban and exurban areas have not been fully utilized. Numerous refuges are located within existing transit service areas, and many have bus or rail stops within walking distance of refuge amenities. However, outside of dense urban areas, visitors use these transit connections infrequently. Reasons for low use include lack of promotion, lack of directions or signage, lack of safe pedestrian infrastructure between transit stop and refuge, and visitors that are unfamiliar with transit use.

Refuges benefit from web-based transit planning tools. New technologies among transit agencies and mapping websites allow visitors to more easily navigate public transit systems to access websites. Several refuge websites include transit directions and links to "Trip Planner" tools on transit agency websites. These directions and tools allow refuges to easily promote transit connections by leveraging existing media.

Transit connections to refuges are multimodal and include shuttle, bus, light rail, heavy rail, and trolley. Existing and potential transit connections also include those serving local destinations, commuters, intra-city transit routes, and inter-city connections. The most common transit mode serving refuges is intra-city bus, and many bus routes offer connections to rail-based transit. Light rail and trolley modes tend to be better promoted by refuge staff.

Transit internal to refuges tends to be seasonal, with successful cases of sharing vehicles between refuges with opposite peak seasons. Tram and shuttle service within refuges often serves an interpretive purpose and caters to groups (students, senior citizens, group homes, and birding and other special interest groups). In a few cases, refuges that house migratory birds in the winter share shuttles with refuges that have peak visitation in the summer. Some refuges send their older vehicles to refuges that want to implement internal transit on a smaller scale.

Refuges are increasingly looking towards alternative fuels for internal transit. Refuges and friends groups that own and operate shuttles or trams within refuges are seeking to purchase vehicles that require less traditional fuel sources. A 2008 FWS Policy and Management Guidance chapter (320) calls for an increase in the use of alternative fuel vehicles.[18] Use of alternative fuels also reduces air pollution and greenhouse gas emissions, further protecting habitat and wildlife. Additionally, many local, state, and federal grant programs offer funds devoted to alternative fuel vehicle acquisition in public agencies.

Trail Findings

Demographic, geographic, and infrastructure quality factors help determine trail use among pedestrians and bicyclists. Bicyclists and pedestrians use trails in different ways, with seasonality, group size, demographics, trail quality, and distances and connections to outlying communities playing important roles. The proximity of nearby communities encourages pedestrian and bicycling use, especially if refuge paths are close to residential neighborhoods or connected to a local or regional trail system. The demographics of nearby communities can also impact the types of visitation seen at refuges; for example younger people may be more likely to engage in recreational activities such as bicycling.

Biking on refuge trails poses a potential conflict with FWS resource protection mission. Unlike visitors on auto tour routes who remain in vehicles, pedestrians and bicyclists can more easily disrupt the habitat of fish, wildlife, and plant resources, especially in areas immediately adjacent to trails. Additionally, wildlife may be startled by the fast speeds that a bicycle can travel. The conflict posed by bicyclists has caused some refuge managers to limit recreational bicycling on refuge trails.

Road infrastructure can be a critical tool to induce bicycle and foot travel. Roadways equipped with bicycle or pedestrian infrastructure are more favorable for encouraging travel via these modes. Infrastructure can include sidewalks, pedestrian crossings, bicycle lanes, and traffic calming measures. These measures tend to slow vehicular speeds or provide dedicated space for bicyclists and pedestrians to navigate. Bicyclists and pedestrians are more likely to travel along a road that they perceive as having lower vehicular speed. Surface quality can also impact the willingness of bicyclists and pedestrians to use roads and sidewalks.

Agency partnerships and community support are key components in facilitating the construction of off-the-road, multi-use trails. Cooperation and partnerships with local communities and operating entities such as recreational and transportation agencies can be a significant obstacle, as coordination with multiple agencies is difficult to achieve. Refuges must also attain community support, especially among neighbors along or near proposed right-of-ways. New trails also should provide ample connections to local roads and other junction points.

Partnerships that exist to support, promote, and further develop multi-use trails are a resource in connecting NWRs to non-motorized infrastructure. National-level groups like the Rails-to-Trails Conservancy play an important role in identifying potential trails, aiding in construction, and supporting and promoting trails to the general public. Local alternative transportation and environmental advocacy groups are also potential partners for refuges in encouraging trail usage. Advocacy groups like these, whether affiliated with refuges or not, are instrumental in cultivating partnerships with refuges and other agencies to host events and advance causes related to recreational trails. The next page profiles a partnership to promote recreational trails between FWS, the Mississippi River Trail, Inc., and other recreational groups along the Mississippi River.

> ### Refuge Access Via Water-Based Transport
>
> Water-based transport offers access to many refuges without the need for a motor vehicle. Refuges located on islands, peninsulas, or coastal areas may be accessible by ferry or located along a "blueway" (a water trail for canoes and kayaks). For example, the Alaska Marine Highway System offers ferry service to or near the Kenai, Kodiak, Alaska Maritime, and Alaska Peninsula NWRs. However, many coastal and island refuges are not open to the public or have limited visitor facilities.

Planning Findings

Regional Transportation Coordinators play the role of facilitator in helping refuges plan projects and acquire funds. RTCs introduce partnerships between refuge staff, advocacy groups, local governments, and elected officials. They also make refuges aware of funding opportunities and benefits that transit and trail projects may bring to local communities.

Staff at the regional and refuge levels have limited capacity to adequately plan for alternative transportation. At the refuge level, many staff members handle multiple responsibilities, including transportation and visitor management. While alternative transportation options can be valuable in realizing refuge goals, transportation considerations may not be prioritized among staff responsibilities, despite the best intentions of refuge managers. RTCs indicated a lack of resources to adequately facilitate transit and trail planning for refuges. The RTCs also face the challenge of staff turnover (both refuge staff and partner agency staff), which results in repetitive education of new staff.[19]

Regional and refuge staff note confusion about eligibility of different entities to obtain Paul S. Sarbanes Transit in the Parks funding. Some regional and refuge staff believe that individual refuges are not allowed to apply for funds, signifying that all applications must go through refuge friends groups. Others encourage individual refuges to apply for Sarbanes grants, with or without the support of friends groups. Eligible grant recipients include individual refuges and state, tribal, or local governments with jurisdiction over land surrounding refuges (or other federal land management areas). Advocacy and friends groups can partner with eligible recipients but cannot receive grant funds.

Local communities and friends and advocacy groups play an active, and sometimes a central, role in bringing about transit and trail connections. Local communities, which stand to benefit from the investment of federal transportation dollars, are often the greatest advocates for trail or transit projects. Several projects emerged directly as a result of community activism. Friends groups also can better communicate with legislative representatives, conduct studies about non-motorized access, and help finance promotional and advertising campaigns in areas where refuge staff are legally restricted from doing so. However, activity levels of friends groups vary by refuge.

Alternative transportation is steadily gaining exposure in the transportation planning process. Alternative transportation can be used as a tool to manage population encroachment near refuges as well as to further the FWS mission to conserve natural resources and meet sustainability goals and greenhouse gas emission reduction goals. Anecdotal experiences with alternative transportation connections at refuges have been positive, and refuge staff members are gaining awareness of the benefits of non-motorized and transit access. RTCs believe that the demand for new connections will increase over the next 10 to 20 years.

Long Range Transportation Plans (LRTPs) and Comprehensive Conservation Plans (CCPs) do not generally include transit and trail connections, but planners increasingly recognize the need to do so. Many refuges did not include alternative transportation as part of their CCP processes, partly because transportation-related guidance for the CCP was only recently released. Regional staff members are beginning to identify refuges where alternative transportation can be an important component of the CCP and are planning to craft CCPs accordingly. The first draft LRTP, in Region 1, has limited inclusions of alternative transportation; FWS staff is working with transportation experts to integrate transit and trail connections into long-range planning.

> ***Mississippi River Connections Collaborative***
>
> The Mississippi River Connections Collaborative (MRCC) involves 32 NWRs, 10 national parks, 8 national scenic and historical trails, and dozens of state parks along the Mississippi River in an effort to develop active transportation corridors along the river. This MOU-based network of partners, along with non-profit organizations such as the Mississippi River Trail, Inc., hopes to pool resources to enhance cultural and interpretive opportunities along the river while maintaining resource restoration and protection. Many refuges along the river, such as the Minnesota Valley (MN) and St. Catherine Creek (MS) NWRs, are working with the MRCC to develop active transportation options and encourage active outdoor lifestyles. The MRCC represents a model effort to use multi-use trails to promote historical and cultural awareness of natural resources, while increasing recreational opportunities through improved visitor access.[19]

Additional Findings

Expanding urban and suburban development may make more refuges accessible via transit and trails in the near future. Refuge staff cites increasing development near refuge boundaries as a major threat to resource protection, and the residents of these developments may bring visitor management challenges as people take advantage of refuge amenities in their neighborhoods. However, transit service areas and non-motorized infrastructure, such as sidewalks and bike lanes, will likely expand alongside developments, putting more refuges within reach of transit service and trails. By leveraging these connections, refuges can reduce vehicle impacts associated with new visitation, such as the need for new parking areas.

Competing funding needs at refuges diverts focus away from alternative transportation investment. RTCs have observed that local, state, and federal funding support for transportation accessing or within refuges is insufficient to meet refuge needs. As such, maintaining adequate trail upkeep and transit service has often taken higher priority over advancing new work.

Transit and trail connections tend to originate organically, based on refuge location. In most cases, strong transit and trail connections occur in urban areas with well-developed transit service and/or extensive non-motorized infrastructure. The connections are usually incidental rather than the product of efforts on behalf of FWS staff and friends groups.

Alternative transportation access to refuges promotes livability, a major focus of the U.S. Department of Transportation. Visitors who can walk, bike, or take transit to refuges can enjoy increased physical activity while reducing air pollution, a benefit that extends to neighboring communities. Also, availability of multiple transportation choices to access refuges fulfills a key principle of livable communities. Livability will likely be a main topic in the upcoming transportation legislation reauthorization.

Recommendations

Based on the findings of this report, FWS Headquarters and regional staff should consider the following recommendations in the areas of promotion, outreach, planning, and transit- and trail-specific recommendations.

Promotion

Establish partnerships with advocacy and friends groups, local governments, transit agencies, and other groups to promote transit and trail connections. These partnerships can increase awareness of non-motorized and transit access as well as increase the use of existing underutilized connections. Refuges may start by working with partners to organize special refuge events that incorporate alternative transportation connections. Refuges can also partner with transit agencies and community groups to promote access to other refuge events. For example, special events can include guided group bicycle and walking tours of refuge sites and organized walks from neighboring towns using existing non-motorized infrastructure.

Enhance promotion of existing transit and trail connections via signage, refuge websites, and advertising. Refuge staff can incorporate simple strategies to promote existing connections. These strategies may include providing links to transit website "Trip Planners" or schedules and maps on refuge websites and on the profiles pages on the NWR's website, posting signs on or near the refuge to orient visitors to trail and transit infrastructure, documenting access options in promotional material and maps, and talking informally about connections with visitors. Staff can also work with partners to install signs in neighboring communities and post advertisements on transit vehicles. While some regions and refuges may identify additional funding and staff capacity needs for promotion, many promotional efforts can be done using existing resources. To be successful with promoting trails and transit access, efforts need to be coordinated with State departments of transportation (DOTs), transit agencies, and trails organizations.

Outreach

Provide greater outreach to RTCs and refuges about the benefits of successful transit and trail connections. Outreach originating at the headquarters level and channeling through RTCs can elevate the level of knowledge about the characteristics of successful connections and help refuge staff recognize opportunities to expand access to their refuges. This outreach can be accomplished through knowledge sharing among RTCs and refuge managers, on-site training, web conferences, facilitated partnerships with transportation planners, and collaboration between transportation staff and outdoor recreation planners. The TRIP Technical Assistance Center and the Volpe Center may be able to provide technical assistance with outreach activities.

Target outreach to clarify funding sources and eligibility for alternative transportation projects. Regional and local staff expressed a lack of clarity regarding funding programs, particularly eligibility to apply for the Sarbanes program. Many refuges were unaware that they could apply directly for Sarbanes program grants. RTCs may also be able to identify other State or local funding sources for non-motorized projects.

Encourage RTCs to work closely with refuge managers and visitor service managers and the TRIP TAC and Volpe to identify opportunities for transit and trail connections as well as potential means of implementation. RTCs are able to uniquely leverage their relationships with refuge staff and knowledge of regional transportation resources to target outreach. RTCs can also help refuge managers to prioritize transportation among refuge management responsibilities and learn how alternative transportation can benefit the refuge.

Planning

Provide greater resources and support to RTCs to help them plan for alternative transportation access. RTCs play the role of facilitator in helping refuges plan projects and acquire funds; they educate refuge staff about available funding opportunities and benefits of transit and trail connections. However, RTCs are hindered by a lack of resources and widespread staff turnover among refuge staff and partner agencies. Dedicated funding and technical assistance for RTCs may expand their capacity to help refuges plan and implement transit and trail connections.

Encourage and provide assistance for the inclusion of alternative transportation in the CCP process. Guidance for transportation components of the CCP is relatively recent and does not explicitly include components on transit and trail access. Headquarters staff may need to work closely with the CCP training staff to ensure that transportation is fully included in CCP training courses. RTCs note that guidance for alternative transportation planning would encourage more refuges to undertake transit and trail connection projects. RTCs may also want to encourage some refuges to pursue a separate transportation study to further examine these issues.

Provide technology, training, assistance, and guidance on how to track changes in visitation levels or experiences following the introduction or improvement of alternative transportation service. RTCs indicated that refuges do not have a mechanism for collecting this information or the resources to conduct data collection. Tracking changes in visitation levels can offer insight into how transit and trail use affects visitation and provide validation for increased investment in alternative transportation projects in the future.

Transit- and Trail-Specific Recommendations

Develop connections between refuges and new and growing communities located near refuge boundaries. Although expanding urban and suburban development presents challenges to refuge resources, refuge staff can proactively address visitor management concerns by developing new alternative transportation connections to refuges. Shifting visitor access to alternative transportation modes could relieve the need for new parking and lessen vehicular impacts upon overtaxed regional and refuge resources. Staff should work with transit agencies, friends groups, local governments, and even private developers to plan non-motorized infrastructure, trail networks, and transit routes that connect visitors with targeted refuge amenities. Without such strategic planning, these connections may develop organically without planning or refuge involvement and potentially lead to conflicts between visitor use and sensitive refuge resources.

Improve and maintain trail surfaces and conditions to ensure they are safe, user-friendly, and comply with the Architectural Barriers Act and the Americans with Disabilities Act. Preserving the quality of multi-use trail surfaces is essential to maintaining visitor use. Uneven surfaces and narrow trails discourage use by cyclists and pedestrians.

Promote bicycle and pedestrian access to coincide with appropriate road infrastructure, utilizing secondary refuge entrances where appropriate. At refuges located along busy roads unsuitable for bicycle or pedestrian use, the best non-motorized connection may be via a secondary refuge entrance.

Encourage bicycling to the refuge even in cases where on-refuge cycling conflicts with the resource protection mission. Some refuges do not permit bicycles on refuge trails due to conflicts with wildlife, and refuge managers are sometimes conflicted about encouraging bicycling as a transportation mode. However, efforts to provide bicycling infrastructure leading to the refuge and promoting bicycling as a transportation mode have helped refuges in reducing the harmful effects of vehicle emissions and improving public health through recreation. Bicycling infrastructure includes safety improvements on feeder roads, connections with or construction of local and regional multi-use trails, an adequate supply of bicycle racks at safe locations, and signage informing of bicycle restrictions on trails.

End Notes

1 FWS data, obtained from *http://www.fws.gov/GIS/data/CadastralDB/index.htm*, features boundaries of FWS land, both acquired and inholding (only acquired lands will be analyzed). Census Bureau data, obtained from *http://www.census.gov/geo/www/cob/ ua2000.html,* features urbanized areas and urban clusters. The Census Bureau defines an urbanized area as consisting of densely settled territory that contains 50,000 or more people and an urbanized cluster as consisting of densely settled territory that has at least 2,500 people and fewer than 50,000 people.

2 The assessment does not specifically analyze rural transit, with the exception of those connections cited by regional staff. Future revisions of this study may investigate rural transit in greater detail.

3 Eastern Federal Lands completed a road safety audit case study for Savannah Pinckney NWR. The results are available at:

http://flh.fhwa.dot.gov/programs/irr/safety/documents/trsa-case-studies-2.pdf.

4 U.S. Census Bureau. 2010. *Population Estimates—Metropolitan and Micropolitan Statistical Areas.* Accessed September 17, 2010, from *http://www.census.gov/popest/metro/files/2009/CBSA-EST2009-alldata.csv.*

5 The Bike Walk Twin Cities website contains links to several bicycle maps and guides:

http://www.bikewalktwincities.org/maps-routes/bike-maps.

6 San Diego Metropolitan Transit System. 2010. *Route 933/934 Timetables.* Accessed September 14, 2010, from

http://www.sdmts.com/home1.asp.

7 San Diego Association of Regional Governments. 2010. *Bayshore Bikeway.* Accessed August 17, 2010, from

http://www.sandag.org/index.asp?projectid=63&fuseaction=projects.detail.

8 U.S. Census Bureau. 2010. *Population Estimates—Metropolitan and Micropolitan Statistical Areas.* Accessed September 17, 2010, from *http://www.census.gov/popest/metro/files/2009/CBSA-EST2009-alldata.csv.*

9 Southeastern Pennsylvania Transportation Authority. 2010. *SEPTA Operating Facts Fiscal Year 2009.* Accessed August 27, 2010, from *http://www.septa.org/reports/pdf/opfacts.pdf.*

10 Clean Air Council. 2007. *A Feasibility Study for Improving Pedestrian and Bicycle Access to John Heinz National Wildlife Refuge.* Accessed August 27, 2010, from *http://www.cleanair.org/Transportation/tfmtrail.html.*

11 Tualatin River National Wildlife Refuge. 2010. "Watchable Wildlife" Brochure. Accessed September 13, 2010, from

http://www.fws.gov/tualatinriver/documents/TualatinRiverNWRwildlifesecure.pdf.

12 Tualatin River National Wildlife Refuge. 2010. *Fact Sheet.* Accessed September 13, 2010, from

http://www.fws.gov/tualatinriver/documents/factsheet10-09.pdf.

13 TriMet. 2010. *Bus Line 12-Barbur/Sandy Blvd Map and Schedule.* Accessed September 13, 2010, from

http://trimet.org/schedules/r012.htm.

14 Trempealeau NWR is managed under the Upper Mississippi River Complex but is not part of the Upper Mississippi River refuge. The study team did not investigate specific transit and trail connections for Trempealeau as part of this study.

15 Wisconsin Department of Natural Resources. 2010. *Great River State Trail.* Accessed September 10, 2010, from

http://dnr.wi.gov/org/land/parks/specific/greatriver/.

16 Upper Mississippi River Fish and Wildlife Refuge. 2010. *Bike Trails.* Accessed September 10, 2010, from

http://www.fws.gov/midwest/uppermississippiriver/biketrails.html.

17 Illinois Department of Natural Resources. 2010. *The Grand Illinois Trail.* Accessed September 10, 2010, from

http://dnr.state.il.us/orep/planning/git.htm.

18 U.S. Fish and Wildlife Service. 2008. *Motor Vehicle Acquisition Planning and Standards.* 320 FW 2. Accessed September 27, 2010, from *www.fws.gov/policy/320fw2.html.*

19 Mississippi River Trail, Inc. 2010. *Mississippi River Connections Collaborative.* Accessed September 27, 2010, from

http://www.mississippirivertrail.org/trails.html.

Appendix

The Transit and Trails matrix was used to tabulate transit and trail rankings for the 142 refuges selected for this study. The study team analyzed each refuge according to the characteristics described in the Backgrounds and Methods section. The team ranked refuges on a scale of one to five based on proximity to urban areas, trail distance, transit distance, trail quality, and transit quality. The matrix contains information on the type of transit service available (light rail, bus), distance from the nearest transit stop to the refuge in miles, name of the local transit agency, names of nearby trails, total length of trails, and distance from the trail to the refuge in miles. Refuge names, addresses, and regions are also included. Each refuge is also qualitatively assessed on the potential for future transit or trail service.

As noted in the Methodology section, the matrix contains only refuges in urban and suburban areas. FWS may benefit from future research to explore rural refuges with connections to rural transit and trails.

Name and Location			Transit			Trails			Rank						Potential	
Refuge	Address	Region	Mode	Distance (Miles)	Transit Agency	Names of Trails	Length of Trail (Miles)	Distance from NWR (Miles)	Urban Area	Transit Distance	Transit Quality	Trail Distance	Trail Quality	Total	Future Transit Potential	Future Trail Potential
STEIGERWALD LAKE NATIONAL WILDLIFE REFUGE	Ridgefield, WA, 98642	1	Bus	About 0 5	C-TRAN	Columbia River Dike Trail	3 5	Adjacent	5	4	3	5	3	20	High	High
TUALATIN RIVER NATIONAL WILDLIFE REFUGE	Sherwood, OR 97140	1	Bus	0.05 / 0.9	Tri-Met				5	5	4	1	1	16	High	
MCNARY NATIONAL WILDLIFE REFUGE	Burbank, WA 99323	1	Bus	5 / 6	Ben Franklin Transit / Amtrak	Benton-Franklin bike/ped trails	Regional system	2	5	1	3	3	4	16	Medium	High
NISQUALLY NATIONAL WILDLIFE REFUGE	Olympia, WA 98516	1	Bus	2	Intercity Transit	Woodland Trail	About 1	4.9	5	1	4	2	2	14	High	Medium
KEALIA POND NATIONAL WILDLIFE REFUGE	Kihei, HI	1	Bus	1.5	Maui Bus				5	2	4	1	1	13		
JAMES CAMPBELL NATIONAL WILDLIFE REFUGE	Hale'iwa, Hawai'i	1	Bus	3.5	The Bus				5	1	4	1	1	12	Medium	
KILAUEA POINT NATIONAL WILDLIFE REFUGE	Kilauea, HI 96754	1	Bus	2	Kauai Bus				5	1	4	1	1	12	High	High
UMATILLA NATIONAL WILDLIFE REFUGE	Umatilla, OR	1				Columbia River Heritage Trail	12	Adjacent	1	1	1	5	4	12		
DEER FLAT NATIONAL WILDLIFE REFUGE	Nampa, ID 83686	1	On-demand Transit		Treasure Valley Transit	Nampa to Stoddard Trail	2	4	5	1	1	2	2	11		
RIDGEFIELD NATIONAL WILDLIFE REFUGE	Ridgefield, WA 98642	1	Bus	12	C-TRAN	Ridgefield Trail System	Planned	Adjacent	1	1	1	5	1	9	High	
ANKENY NATIONAL WILDLIFE REFUGE	Jefferson, OR 97352	1	Bus	10	Cherriots				1	1	2	1	1	6		
WILLIAM L. FINLEY NATIONAL WILDLIFE REFUGE	Corvallis, OR 97333	1	Bus	12.6	City of Corvallis Transit				1	1	2	1	1	6		
BASKETT SLOUGH NATIONAL WILDLIFE REFUGE	Dallas, OR 97338	1	None						1	1	1	1	1	5		
WICHITA MOUNTAINS WILDLIFE REFUGE	Indiahoma, OK	2				Planned			1	1	1	5	3	11	High	High

Name and Location			Transit			Trails			Rank						Potential	
Refuge	Address	Region	Mode	Distance (Miles)	Transit Agency	Names of Trails	Length of Trail (Miles)	Distance from NWR (Miles)	Urban Area	Transit Distance	Transit Quality	Trail Distance	Trail Quality	Total	Future Transit Potential	Future Trail Potential
LAGUNA ATASCOSA NATIONAL WILDLIFE REFUGE	Los Fresnos, TX 78566	2	Internal tram						5	1	1	1	1	9		
LOWER RIO GRANDE VALLEY NATIONAL WILDLIFE REFUGE	Alamo, TX 78516	2	None						5	1	1	1	1	9		
SAN ANDRES NATIONAL WILDLIFE REFUGE	Refuge closed to the public	2	None						5	1	1	1	1	9		
BALCONES CANYONLANDS NATIONAL WILDLIFE REFUGE	Marble Falls, TX 78654	2	Bus	5.5	Capital Metro				1	1	3	1	1	7		
BOSQUE DEL APACHE NATIONAL WILDLIFE REFUGE	San Antonio, NM	2	Train	10 miles	New Mexico Rail Runner				1	1	3	1	1	7		
SANTA ANA NATIONAL WILDLIFE REFUGE	Alamo, Texas 78516	2	NONE	Internal	Texas Parks & Wildlife				1	1	1	1	1	5		
MINNESOTA VALLEY NATIONAL WILDLIFE REFUGE	Bloomington, MN	3	Light Rail	0.4	Metro	Most are unnamed trails running along Mississippi and Minnesota Rivers; Southwest Regional LRT- South Corridor is an NRT	Varies; Southwest Regional LRT is 27 miles	Most run within; Southwest Regional LRT runs adjacent at end	5	4	5	5	5	24		
BIG MUDDY NATIONAL FISH AND WILDLIFE REFUGE	Columbia, MO 65201	3	None			Katy Trail State Park	225	Within different units	5	1	1	5	5	17		
UPPER MISSISSIPPI RIVER NATIONAL WILDLIFE AND FISH REFUGE-SAVANNA DISTRICT	Thomson, IL	3				Great River Trail	60	Within	5	1	1	5	5	17		

Refuge	Address	Region	Mode	Distance (Miles)	Transit Agency	Names of Trails	Length of Trail (Miles)	Distance from NWR (Miles)	Urban Area	Transit Distance	Transit Quality	Trail Distance	Trail Quality	Total	Future Transit Potential	Future Trail Potential
UPPER MISSISSIPPI RIVER NATIONAL WILDLIFE AND FISH REFUGE-LA CROSSE DISTRICT	Onalaska, WI	3			LaCrosse Municipal Transit Utility; Onalaska Shared Ride Taxi	La Crosse River State Trail/Great River State Trail	21/24	3.1/Within	5	1	1	5	4	16		
DETROIT RIVER INTERNATIONAL WILDLIFE REFUGE	Grosse Ile, MI 48138	3	Bus	<2	SMART	Kennedy Park Trail; Elizabeth Park Trail/ Unnamed Trail in Woodhaven	Ap. 1.5/ 0.75/Ap. 1 2	1.8/2/4	5	3	3	2	2	15		
SHIAWASSEE NATIONAL WILDLIFE REFUGE	Saginaw, MI 48601	3	Bus	0.6	Saginaw Transit Authority Regional Service	Saginaw Valley Rail Trail/unnamed	7 5/2	Within/3.6	5	3	3	1	1	13	Low	Low
BOYER CHUTE NATIONAL WILDLIFE REFUGE	3720 Rivers Way, Ft. Calhoun, NE 68023	3	Bus	9.8	Metro Area Transit (Omaha)	John J. Pershing Drive/N. River Rd.	About 3?	Connects	1	1	3	5	2	12		Medium
SENEY NATIONAL WILDLIFE REFUGE	Seney, MI	3	Internal shuttle bus						1	5	2	1	1	10		
MIDDLE MISSISSIPPI RIVER NATIONAL WILDLIFE REFUGE	Rockwood, IL 62280	3							5	1	1	1	1	9		
UPPER MISSISSIPPI RIVER NATIONAL WILDLIFE AND FISH REFUGE-MCGREGOR DISTRICT	McGregor, IA	3							5	1	1	1	1	9		
OTTAWA NATIONAL WILDLIFE REFUGE	Oak Harbor, OH 43449	3	Internal shuttle bus						3	1	1	1	1	7	Medium	
UPPER MISSISSIPPI RIVER NATIONAL WILDLIFE AND FISH REFUGE-WINONA DISTRICT	Winona, MN 55987	3			City of Winona Transit Services; Houston City Bus / Hurricane Express	Great River State Trail	24	Within	3	1	1	1	1	7		
HORICON NATIONAL WILDLIFE REFUGE	Mayville, WI 53050	3	None			Wild Goose State Trail	34	Within	1	1	1	1	1	5		
NEAL SMITH NATIONAL WILDLIFE REFUGE	Prairie City, IA 50228	3	NONE			Bike Trail			1	1	1	1	1	5		Medium

U. S. Fish & Wildlife Service

Name and Location		Transit				Trails			Rank						Potential	
Refuge	Address	Region	Mode	Distance (Miles)	Transit Agency	Names of Trails	Length of Trail (Miles)	Distance from NWR (Miles)	Urban Area	Transit Distance	Transit Quality	Trail Distance	Trail Quality	Total	Future Transit Potential	Future Trail Potential
BIG BRANCH MARSH NATIONAL WILDLIFE REFUGE	61389 Hwy. 434, Lacombe, LA 70445	4	None			Tammany Trace	27.5	Adjacent	5	1	1	5	4	16		
PELICAN ISLAND NATIONAL WILDLIFE REFUGE	1339 20th St, Vero Beach, FL 32960	4	Bus	12	GoLineIRT	Jungle Trail	7 8	Through refuge	5	1	2	5	3	16		
ARCHIE CARR NATIONAL WILDLIFE REFUGE	1339 20th St, Vero Beach, FL 32960	4	Bus	5	Space Coast Area Transit	Jungle Trail	7 8	0.5	5	1	2	4	3	15		
J.N. 'DING' DARLING NATIONAL WILDLIFE REFUGE	1 Wildlife Drive, Sanibel, FL	4	None			Surfsound Ct/Locke Ave/unnamed	All <0.5 miles	Adjacent	5	1	1	5	3	15		
LAKE WOODRUFF NATIONAL WILDLIFE REFUGE	2045 Mud Lake Road, Deleon Springs, FL 32130	4	Bus	0.8 ?	VOTRAN				5	4	2	1	1	13		
MOUNTAIN LONGLEAF NATIONAL WILDLIFE REFUGE	P.O. Box 5087, Fort McClellan, AL 36205	4	Bus	5	Areawide Community Transportation System (Anniston, AL)	Chief Ladiga Trail	33	4.3	5	1	1	2	4	13		
ARTHUR R. MARSHALL LOXAHATCHEE NATIONAL WILDLIFE REFUGE	10216 Lee Road, Boynton Beach, FL 33437	4	Bus and Rail	7 / 11.5	PalmTran and Tri-Rail				5	1	3	1	1	11		
BAYOU SAUVAGE NATIONAL WILDLIFE REFUGE	61389 Hwy. 434, Lacombe, LA 70445	4	Bus	4.5	NORTA				5	1	3	1	1	11		
MISSISSIPPI SANDHILL CRANE NATIONAL WILDLIFE REFUGE	7200 Crane Lane, Gautier, MS 39553	4	Bus	1.5 (approx.)	Coast Transit				5	2	2	1	1	11		
HOBE SOUND NATIONAL WILDLIFE REFUGE	P.O. Box 645, Hobe Sound, FL 33475	4	Bus	8	PalmTran				5	1	2	1	1	10		
MERRITT ISLAND NATIONAL WILDLIFE REFUGE	State Hwy 402, Titusville, FL 32782	4	Bus	5.9	Space Coast Area Transit				5	1	2	1	1	10		
RED RIVER NATIONAL WILDLIFE REFUGE	555 Sunflower Road, Bossier City, LA	4	Bus	4	SPORTRAN				5	2	1	1	1	10	High	

U. S. Fish & Wildlife Service

Refuge	Address	Region	Mode	Distance (Miles)	Transit Agency	Names of Trails	Length of Trail (Miles)	Distance from NWR (Miles)	Urban Area	Transit Distance	Transit Quality	Trail Distance	Trail Quality	Total	Future Transit Potential	Future Trail Potential
ST. MARKS NATIONAL WILDLIFE REFUGE	1255 Lighthouse Road, St. Marks FL 32355	4	NONE			Tallahassee-St. Marks Historic Railroad Trail	20	2	1	1	1	2	5	10		
BLACK BAYOU LAKE NATIONAL WILDLIFE REFUGE	480 Richland Place, Monroe, LA	4	Bus	7					5	1	1	1	1	9		
CALOOSAHATCHEE NATIONAL WILDLIFE REFUGE	Closed to the public	4							5	1	1	1	1	9		
D'ARBONNE NATIONAL WILDLIFE REFUGE	11372 Hwy 143, Farmerville, LA 71241	4	Bus?		Monroe Transit System				5	1	1	1	1	9		
LAGUNA CARTAGENA NATIONAL WILDLIFE REFUGE	PO Box 510, Boquerón, PR 00622	4	None						5	1	1	1	1	9		
LAKE WALES RIDGE NATIONAL WILDLIFE REFUGE	Closed to the public	4							5	1	1	1	1	9		
MANDALAY NATIONAL WILDLIFE REFUGE	3599 Bayou Black Drive, Houma, LA 70360	4	None						5	1	1	1	1	9		
NATIONAL KEY DEER REFUGE	28950 Watson Blvd., Big Pine Key, FL 33043; 209 Key Deer Blvd (Visitor Center)	4	Intercity bus	0-2.5	Greyhound				3	3	1	1	1	9		
PINELLAS NATIONAL WILDLIFE REFUGE	Closed to the public	4	None						5	1	1	1	1	9		
SAVANNAH-PINCKNEY NATIONAL WILDLIFE REFUGES	694 BEECH HILL LANE HARDEEVILLE, GEORGIA 29927 (Refuge near Hilton Head Island, SC)	4	Bus	Unknown	Lowcountry Regional Transit Authority				5	1	1	1	1	9		
ST. JOHNS NATIONAL WILDLIFE REFUGE	Off Hwy 50 west of Titusville, FL, Titusville, FL 32752 - NO PUBLIC ACCESS	4							5	1	1	1	1	9		
WACCAMAW NATIONAL WILDLIFE REFUGE	1601 N. Fraser St. Georgetown, SC 29440	4	None						5	1	1	1	1	9		

| Name and Location | | Region | Transit | | | Trails | | | Rank | | | | | | Potential | |
Refuge	Address		Mode	Distance (Miles)	Transit Agency	Names of Trails	Length of Trail (Miles)	Distance from NWR (Miles)	Urban Area	Transit Distance	Transit Quality	Trail Distance	Trail Quality	Total	Future Transit Potential	Future Trail Potential
WASSAW NATIONAL WILDLIFE REFUGE	Only accessible by boat	4							5	1	1	1	1	9		
WATERCRESS DARTER NATIONAL WILDLIFE REFUGE	Limited public use due to small size of refuge and endangered species	4	On-demand rural transit		MCATS - Morgan County Area Transportation System; TRAM - Transportation for Rural Areas of Madison County				5	1	1	1	1	9		
WHEELER NATIONAL WILDLIFE REFUGE	2700 Refuge Headquarters Rd., Decatur, AL 35603	4							5	1	1	1	1	9		
ALLIGATOR RIVER NATIONAL WILDLIFE REFUGE	708 N. Hwy 64, Manteo, NC	4	None						3	1	1	1	1	7		
BAYOU TECHE NATIONAL WILDLIFE REFUGE	10816A Hwy 182 E, Franklin, LA 70538	4							3	1	1	1	1	7		
GREAT WHITE HERON NATIONAL WILDLIFE REFUGE	28590 Watson Blvd, Big Pine Key, FL 33043	4							3	1	1	1	1	7		
KEY WEST NATIONAL WILDLIFE REFUGE	28590 Watson Blvd, Big Pine Key, FL 33043	4							3	1	1	1	1	7		
FELSENTHAL NATIONAL WILDLIFE REFUGE	5531 Hwy 82 West, Crossett, AR 41635	4							1	1	1	1	1	5		
GRAND BAY NATIONAL WILDLIFE REFUGE	6005 Bayou Heron Road, Moss Point, MS 39562	4							1	1	1	1	1	5		
HANDY BRAKE NATIONAL WILDLIFE REFUGE	11372 Hwy 143, Farmerville, LA 71241	4							1	1	1	1	1	5		
MATTAMUSKEET NATIONAL WILDLIFE REFUGE	38 Mattamuskeet Rd, Swan Quarter, NC 27885	4							1	1	1	1	1	5		

| Name and Location | | | Transit | | | Trails | | | Rank | | | | | | Potential | |
Refuge	Address	Region	Mode	Distance (Miles)	Transit Agency	Names of Trails	Length of Trail (Miles)	Distance from NWR (Miles)	Urban Area	Transit Distance	Transit Quality	Trail Distance	Trail Quality	Total	Future Transit Potential	Future Trail Potential
OVERFLOW NATIONAL WILDLIFE REFUGE	3858 Hwy 8 E, Parkdale, AR 71661	4							1	1	1	1	1	5		
PEA ISLAND NATIONAL WILDLIFE REFUGE	Manteo, NC	4							1	1	1	1	1	5		
POCOSIN LAKES NATIONAL WILDLIFE REFUGE	Columbia, NC 27925	4							1	1	1	1	1	5		
ST. CATHERINE CREEK NATIONAL WILDLIFE REFUGE	76 Pintail Lane, Sibley, MS 39165	4	Internal tram						1	1	1	1	1	5		
SWANQUARTER NATIONAL WILDLIFE REFUGE	38 Mattamuskeet Rd, Swan Quarter, NC 27885	4							1	1	1	1	1	5		
UPPER OUACHITA NATIONAL WILDLIFE REFUGE	11372 Hwy 143, Farmerville, LA 71241	4							1	1	1	1	1	5		
JOHN HEINZ NATIONAL WILDLIFE REFUGE AT TINICUM	8601 Lindbergh Blvd, Philadelphia, PA 19153	5	Bus and Train	0.3 - 0.8 (1.5 for R2 line)	SEPTA	Unnamed		Within	5	4	5	5	2	21		
ASSABET RIVER NATIONAL WILDLIFE REFUGE	73 Weir Hill Rd, Sudbury, MA 01776	5	Rail	7.5	MBTA	Assabet River Rail Trail/White Pond Rd. Trail	5.6/approx. 2	Both run through/ WPRT completely within	5	1	2	5	4	17		
CAPE MAY NATIONAL WILDLIFE REFUGE	24 Kimbles Beach Road, Cape May Court House, NJ 08210	5	Bus	3.5	NJ Transit	Middle Township Bike Path	1.1	3.1	5	1	3	3	2	14		
JOHN H. CHAFEE NATIONAL WILDLIFE REFUGE	Narragansett/South Kingstown, RI 02882	5	None			William C. O'Neill Bike Path	6.1	0.5	5	1	1	4	3	14		
MONOMOY NATIONAL WILDLIFE REFUGE	73 Weir Hill Road, Sudbury, MA 01776 (NWR is near Chatham, MA)	5	Bus	2.7	Cape Cod Regional Transit Authority	Cape Cod Rail Trail	22	4.8	5	1	2	2	4	14	High	High

| Name and Location | | Transit | | | | Trails | | | Rank | | | | | | Potential | |
Refuge	Address	Region	Mode	Distance (Miles)	Transit Agency	Names of Trails	Length of Trail (Miles)	Distance from NWR (Miles)	Urban Area	Transit Distance	Transit Quality	Trail Distance	Trail Quality	Total	Future Transit Potential	Future Trail Potential
OCCOQUAN BAY NATIONAL WILDLIFE REFUGE	13950 Dawson Beach Rd, Woodbridge, VA 22191	5	Rail / Bus	0.6	Amtrak Northeast Regional / Potomac and Rappahannock Transportation Commission				5	3	4	1	1	14		
WERTHEIM NATIONAL WILDLIFE REFUGE	360 Smith Road, Shirley, NY 11967	5	Train / bus	0.9 / stops at entrance	LIRR / Suffolk County Transit				5	4	3	1	1	14		
EDWIN B. FORSYTHE NATIONAL WILDLIFE REFUGE	800 Great Creek Road, Oceanville, NJ 08231	5	Bus	0.8	NJ Transit	Barnegat Branch Trail	2 miles	0	5	3	3	1	1	13		Medium
PATUXENT RESEARCH REFUGE	10901 Scarlet Tanager Loop, Laurel, MD 20708	5	Rail	3.2 - 7.5	MARC	Washington Baltimore and Annapolis Trail- PG County	6 2	3.5	5	1	2	2	3	13	Medium	Medium
GREAT SWAMP NATIONAL WILDLIFE REFUGE	241 Pleasant Plains Road, Basking Ridge, NJ 07920	5	Rail	3.5-4.5	NJ Transit	Tracton Line Recreation Trail	3 2	2.5	5	1	4	1	1	12		High
WALLKILL RIVER NATIONAL WILDLIFE REFUGE	1547 County Route 565, Sussex, NJ	5	Bus	<0.25	Sussex County Skylands Ride				3	5	2	1	1	12		
CHINCOTEAGUE NATIONAL WILDLIFE REFUGE	8231 Beach Rd., Chincoteague, VA 23336	5	Trolley	1.2	Town of Chincoteague Island Trolley				3	2	4	1	1	11	High	High
GREAT MEADOWS NATIONAL WILDLIFE REFUGE	73 Weir Hill Road, Sudbury, MA 01776	5	Rail	4.2	MBTA	Reformatory Branch Trail/Bedford Narrow Gauge RT/Minuteman Bikeway/Bruce Freeman RT		0/3.1/2.8/8 5	5	1	3	1	1	11	Medium	Medium
SEATUCK NATIONAL WILDLIFE REFUGE	500 St. Marks Ln, Islip, NY - CLOSED TO PUBLIC	5							5	1	3	1	1	11		
STEWART B. MCKINNEY NATIONAL WILDLIFE REFUGE	733 Old Clinton Road, Westbrook, CT 06498	5	Bus	1.2	Estuary Transit				5	2	2	1	1	11		

U. S. Fish & Wildlife Service

Refuge	Address	Region	Mode	Distance (Miles)	Transit Agency	Names of Trails	Length of Trail (Miles)	Distance from NWR (Miles)	Urban Area	Transit Distance	Transit Quality	Trail Distance	Trail Quality	Total	Future Transit Potential	Future Trail Potential
SUNKHAZE MEADOWS NATIONAL WILDLIFE REFUGE	16 Rockport Park Centre, Rockport, ME (refuge actually located in Milford, ME)	5	Bus	7	BAT Community Connector				5	1	3	1	1	11		
AMAGANSETT NATIONAL WILDLIFE REFUGE	Atlantic Ave, Amagansett, NY 11930	5	Train	0.9	Long Island Railroad				3	3	2	1	1	10		
BACK BAY NATIONAL WILDLIFE REFUGE	4005 Sandpiper Road, Virginia Beach, VA 23456	5	Bus	12	HRTransit				5	1	2	1	1	10		
GREAT BAY NATIONAL WILDLIFE REFUGE	100 Merrimac Drive, Newington, NH 03801	5	Bus	3	COAST				5	1	2	1	1	10	Medium	
OXBOW NATIONAL WILDLIFE REFUGE	Still River Depot Rd., Harvard, MA 01451	5	Commuter rail	2-5	MBTA	Nashua River Rail Trail	12.3	1.9	5	1	2	1	1	10		Medium
PARKER RIVER NATIONAL WILDLIFE REFUGE	261 Northern Blvd, Plum Island, Newburyport, MA 01950	5	Commuter rail	8.7	MBTA				5	1	2	1	1	10		Medium
RACHEL CARSON NATIONAL WILDLIFE REFUGE	321 Port Road, Wells, ME	5	Rail	4.1	Amtrak Downeaster				5	1	2	1	1	10		
CONSCIENCE POINT NATIONAL WILDLIFE REFUGE	N/A (in North Sea, NY)	5	None						5	1	1	1	1	9		
FEATHERSTONE NATIONAL WILDLIFE REFUGE	Closed to the public	5	None						5	1	1	1	1	9		
GREAT DISMAL SWAMP NWR	3100 Desert Road, Suffolk, VA 23434	5	None						5	1	1	1	1	9		
LIDO BEACH WILDLIFE MANAGEMENT AREA	Closed to the public	5							5	1	1	1	1	9		
MASHPEE NATIONAL WILDLIFE REFUGE	Refuge closed to the public	5	None						5	1	1	1	1	9		
MASSASOIT NATIONAL WILDLIFE REFUGE	Refuge closed to the public	5	None						5	1	1	1	1	9		

| Name and Location | | Transit | | | | Trails | | | Rank | | | | | | Potential | |
Refuge	Address	Region	Mode	Distance (Miles)	Transit Agency	Names of Trails	Length of Trail (Miles)	Distance from NWR (Miles)	Urban Area	Transit Distance	Transit Quality	Trail Distance	Trail Quality	Total	Future Transit Potential	Future Trail Potential
OHIO RIVER ISLANDS NATIONAL WILDLIFE REFUGE	3982 Waverly Road, Williamstown, WV 26187	5	None	2.6	Washington-Morgan Community Action				5	1	1	1	1	9		
OYSTER BAY NATIONAL WILDLIFE REFUGE	Only accessible by boat	5	NONE						5	1	1	1	1	9		
PLUM TREE ISLAND NATIONAL WILDLIFE REFUGE	Closed to the public	5	None						5	1	1	1	1	9		
SUPAWNA MEADOWS NATIONAL WILDLIFE REFUGE	197 Lighthouse Road, Pennsville, NJ	5	None						5	1	1	1	1	9		
TRUSTOM POND NATIONAL WILDLIFE REFUGE	1040 Matunuck Schoolhouse Road, South Kingstown, RI 02879	5	NONE						5	1	1	1	1	9		
BLOCK ISLAND NATIONAL WILDLIFE REFUGE	New Shoreham, RI 02807	5	Ferry	4.1	Long Island Ferry, Block Island Ferry				1	1	2	1	1	6		
CANAAN VALLEY NATIONAL WILDLIFE REFUGE	Davis, WV	5				Blackwater Canyon NRT	10	8	1	1	1	1	2	6		
TARGET ROCK NATIONAL WILDLIFE REFUGE	12 Target Rock Rd., Huntington, NY 11743	5	Trail	9.2	LIRR				1	1	2	1	1	6		
BLACKWATER NATIONAL WILDLIFE REFUGE	2145 Key Wallace Dr, Cambridge, MD	5	Bus	11	Delmarva Community Transit				1	1	1	1	1	5		
EASTERN NECK NATIONAL WILDLIFE REFUGE	1730 Eastern Neck Rd, Rock Hall, MD 21661	5	Bus	8	Delmarva Community Transit				1	1	1	1	1	5		
EASTERN SHORE OF VIRGINIA NATIONAL WILDLIFE REFUGE	5003 Hallett Circle, Cape Charles, VA, 23310	5							1	1	1	1	1	5		Medium
ELIZABETH ALEXANDRA MORTON NATIONAL WILDLIFE REFUGE	784 Noyack Rd, Sag Harbor, NY 11963	5							1	1	1	1	1	5		

Refuge	Address	Region	Mode	Distance (Miles)	Transit Agency	Names of Trails	Length of Trail (Miles)	Distance from NWR (Miles)	Urban Area	Transit Distance	Transit Quality	Trail Distance	Trail Quality	Total	Future Transit Potential	Future Trail Potential
MASON NECK NATIONAL WILDLIFE REFUGE	7603 High Point Rd, Lorton, VA 22079	5	Train	6	Amtrak				1	1	1	1	1	5		
NANTUCKET NATIONAL WILDLIFE REFUGE	73 Weir Hill Road, Sudbury MA	5	NONE						1	1	1	1	1	5		
NINIGRET NATIONAL WILDLIFE REFUGE	50 Bend Road, Charlestown RI 02813	5	NONE						1	1	1	1	1	5		
SACHUEST POINT NATIONAL WILDLIFE REFUGE	769 Sachuest Point Road, Middletown RI 02842	5	NONE						1	1	1	1	1	5		
ROCKY MOUNTAIN ARSENAL NATIONAL WILDLIFE REFUGE	7200 Quebec St, Commerce City, CO 80022	6	Bus	0.5 - 1	RTD-Denver	-Perimeter Trail -Sand Creek Regional Greenway -E. 70th St. -Second Creek Trail	19 13 1.25 4 5	Adjacent 2.5 2.3 Adjacent	5	3	3	5	5	21	High	High
TWO PONDS NATIONAL WILDLIFE REFUGE	7200 Quebec St, Commerce City, CO 80022	6	Bus	0.5 / 1.1	RTD-Denver		Vary from <1 to 6-7	Closest is a little more than mile away	5	4	4	3	4	20	High	
NATIONAL ELK REFUGE	Jackson, WY	6				Under construction	15		3	1	1	5	5	15		High
BOWDOIN NATIONAL WILDLIFE REFUGE	194 Bowdoin Auto Tour Road, Malta, MT 59538	6	Rail	8	Amtrak Empire Builder				1	3	2	1	1	8		
ALAMOSA NATIONAL WILDLIFE REFUGE	9383 El Rancho Lane, Alamosa, CO 81101	6							3	1	1	1	1	7		High
BENTON LAKE NATIONAL WILDLIFE REFUGE	922 Bootlegger Trail, Great Falls, MT 59404	6	Bus	10+	Great Falls Transit District				1	1	2	1	1	6	Low	
LEE METCALF NATIONAL WILDLIFE REFUGE	4567 Wildfowl Lane, Stevensville, MT 59870	6	None						1	1	1	1	1	5		Medium
KENAI NATIONAL WILDLIFE REFUGE	Ski Hill Rd, PO Box 2139, Soldotna, AK 99669	7							3	1	1	1	1	7	Low	Low

Name and Location			Transit			Trails			Rank						Potential	
Refuge	Address	Region	Mode	Distance (Miles)	Transit Agency	Names of Trails	Length of Trail (Miles)	Distance from NWR (Miles)	Urban Area	Transit Distance	Transit Quality	Trail Distance	Trail Quality	Total	Future Transit Potential	Future Trail Potential
KODIAK NATIONAL WILDLIFE REFUGE	1390 Buskin River Rd, Kodiak, AK 99615	7							1	1	1	1	1	5	Low	Low
SAN DIEGO BAY NATIONAL WILDLIFE REFUGE	Chula Vista, CA 91910	1	Shuttle bus	0	Chula Vista Transit Authority	Unnamed/Bayshore Bikeway (Silver Strand Bikeway)	About 2.5/12	0.6/3.8	5	5	4	4	5	23		
TIJUANA SLOUGH NATIONAL WILDLIFE REFUGE	301 Caspian Way, Imperial Beach, CA 91932	8	Bus	0.1	MTS	Bayshore Bikeway (Silver Strand Bikeway)	12	1.6	5	5	4	3	5	22		
DON EDWARDS SAN FRANCISCO BAY NATIONAL WILDLIFE REFUGE	9500 Thornton Ave., Newark, CA 94560	8	Bus	1	Alameda - Contra Costa Transit	Mostly unnamed; Coyote Hills Regional Park Trail System	Varies- <0 5 miles to 10	Within	5	2	3	5	4	19		
ANTIOCH DUNES NATIONAL WILDLIFE REFUGE	Contra Costa County, CA	8	Train / bus	1.5 / 0 2	Amtrak / Tri Delta Transit	Contra Costa Trail; unnamed	Approx. 8; Approx. 12	Each about 3.6 miles away	5	4	4	2	3	18		
SEAL BEACH NATIONAL WILDLIFE REFUGE	800 Seal Beach Blvd., Seal Beach, CA - ON A MILITARY BASE, VERY LIMITED PUBLIC ACCESS	8	None			San Gabriel River Trail	38	1.8	5	1	1	3	5	15		
STONE LAKES NATIONAL WILDLIFE REFUGE	1624 Hood-Franklin Road, Elk Grove, CA 95757	8	Bus	2.1	Sacramento Regional Transit				5	1	2	1	1	10		
COACHELLA VALLEY NATIONAL WILDLIFE REFUGE	Off Interstate 10 at the Cook St exit, Riverside, CA	8	None						5	1	1	1	1	9		
DESERT NATIONAL WILDLIFE RANGE	16001 Corn Creek Rd, Las Vegas, NV 89124	8	None						5	1	1	1	1	9		
ELLICOTT SLOUGH NATIONAL WILDLIFE REFUGE	Closed to the public	8	None						5	1	1	1	1	9		
MARIN ISLANDS NATIONAL WILDLIFE REFUGE	Closed to the public	8							5	1	1	1	1	9		
NORTH CENTRAL VALLEY WILDLIFE MANAGEMENT AREA	Closed to the public	8							5	1	1	1	1	9		
SAN DIEGO NATIONAL WILDLIFE REFUGE	14715 Hwy 94, Jamul, CA 91935	8							5	1	1	1	1	9